My Last Rock Bottom

My Last Rock Bottom

Sara Berelsman

2ⁿᵈ Edition

2015

Marble, NC USA

Copyright © 2013 Word Branch Publishing

Second Editions copyright © 2015

All rights reserved. This book or any portion thereof may not be reproduced or used in any manner whatsoever without the express written permission of the publisher except for the use of brief quotations in a book review.
This is a work of fiction. Names, characters, businesses, places, events and incidents are either the products of the author's imagination or used in a fictitious manner. Any resemblance to actual persons, living or dead, or actual events is purely coincidental.

Printed in the USA

Cover illustration © 2013 Julian Norwood

Permission can be obtained for re-use of portions of material by writing to the address below. Some permission requests can be granted free of charge, others carry a fee.

Word Branch Publishing
PO Box 41
Marble, NC 28905

http://wordbranch.com
sales@wordbranch.com

Library of Congress Control Number: 20139210008

ISBN-13: 978-0692382349
ISBN-10: 0692382348

For Andy, who stayed with me even when I was the biggest asshole on the planet.

What Readers Are Saying about *My Last Rock Bottom*

"It's actually fabulous. [Sara] understands how honesty affects people and she is really willing to go there." Stefanie Wilder-Taylor: Comedian and Author

~~~

"There's so much rawness in this book. It took a lot of courage and bravery to be so honest." Carla

~~~

"This book gives you hope that things do get better for you, once you start getting honest with yourself." Lisa

~~~

"Your voice has made at least one person in the world feel not alone. Thank you from the bottom of my heart." Narupa

~~~

"Honest and raw, it's hard to say painful things but Sara did it well." Stacey

~~~

"This book was truly heartwarming, I felt as if I've known Sara my whole life. Her experiences are raw and powerful, and she's a hero for opening up to the world about her struggles." Brittani

Note to Readers

This book is for mature readers and contains some sexual content and bad language. I've changed names to protect identities. A lot of the book takes place in the past, and the way people are described is not necessarily how they are now. Keep in mind this was written from what I remember, and I was drunk a lot.

If you're ready to criticize me to shreds by the end, please remember: I'm a recovering alcoholic.

I'm fragile.

Sara Berelsman

Table of Contents

That Night 1
In the Beginning 3
The End of Ben 7
Factory Man 15
The Bodybuilder 23
My Least Favorite Mistake 31
The Decision 41
The Rose 45
What to Expect When You Are Unexpectedly Expecting 49
I Walked the Line 55
Emotional Nuptials 61
And Then There Were Four 65
Gasoline Rainbows 69
The Panic Attack 77
My Last Rock Bottom 91
The Light 97
The Sobriety Diaries 101
    (10/16/11) 101
    (10/30/11) 103
    (11/1/11) 106
    (11/6/11) 108
The Meeting 117

Finding Myself Sober 119

The Diagnosis 123

Eyes Wide Open 127

Giving Thanks 137

Black Friday . . . Indeed 139

The After Party 143

Breaking Up Is Hard to Do 147

Day by Day 155

A Magical Year 161

Reality Check 165

Coming Out of the Darkness 167

Wishing on Dandelions 169

That Night

Scratches covered my body. They were up and down my arms and legs, some more intense than others, threatening to break through the skin and bleed. My daughter had them too. I had bruises everywhere, and I had no idea why or how. I couldn't find my shirt. It was morning, but what time was it?

I made it home, feeling as if I'd fought in some sort of war, attempting to put the pieces together of the night before in a way that my husband would understand…that I would understand.

I didn't understand.

I remembered the wine. The pills. More wine. More pills. It was raining outside. We were laughing. I remembered the bathtub. The giant bathtub. With lots of bubbles. I remembered being so out of it, blacking out and then reappearing for seconds at a time, catching glimpses of skin and bubbles.

What happened?

Once the longest, most painful hangover of my life started to set in, I started putting pieces together about what had occurred that drunken Thursday night and the morning after, the morning I'd come home covered in scratches.

The alarm clock had startled us that morning. Six a.m.

We were still drinking.

It was sunrise. I had to drive home from my friends' house with my children in the car.

I must've fallen into their rose bushes while holding my youngest daughter, which explains the scratches up and down our arms and legs. Waves of guilt washed over me when I discovered this. I was officially the worst mother alive. I wanted to die.

I drove home completely blacked out. I got there okay somehow, feeling as if I'd been hit by a train. I was still completely drunk.

After falling into bed that morning next to my patiently waiting husband, I knew I had to do something.

I went to the back porch and sat, hugging my knees to my chest. I was rocking back and forth on the concrete as the tears began to fall, hot and unforgiving. I called my therapist to tell him what happened. I was crying so hard he could barely understand me.

I couldn't stop sobbing.

In the Beginning

All things truly wicked start from innocence. ~ *Ernest Hemingway*

In order for the present to make sense, one often has to return to the past. It's so weird, if you think about it. What it is. Why people buy it and partake in it. Individuals consume most food and drinks because they like the taste. Not alcohol. At least, not some of the time. We buy alcohol by the truckload with one purpose in mind: to feel good. To not feel anything for a while. To escape. We imbibe in this substance, drink down this liquid in various flavors, drink as much of it in a night as we can, in order to feel good. It's a ritual. It's very strange. The next day we generally feel awful, barely making it through the day, mostly lying on the couch attempting to alleviate the hangover and worst pounding headache on the planet.

This was my life.

It's strange. So very, very strange. What's even more strange, however, is the way this curious liquid has the power to morph us into different human beings than we might normally be, and cause us to interact in ways we normally wouldn't. Compel us to make decisions we'd never make sober. Yet somehow we continue this drinking ritual over and over. As much as it has the power to cause pain, it primarily relieves it – if only temporarily. At least, it did mine. It relieved my pain until I realized, finally, it was causing more pain than it was masking.

It's amazing, really, the lies we tell ourselves so we can behave in every way imaginable in order to avoid feeling any pain. In order to avoid feeling anything at all. That's all I wanted, every day. To feel good. To feel happy. To exist on a higher plane where depression had no place. When I drank, I felt good. I felt great! This goes without mentioning the consequences of said drinking, however. All I know is, when I was drunk, I was fine. Or so I thought.

My first drink was in the third grade. Don't be alarmed; I wasn't a regular boozer, inebriated while riding bikes or playing dress-up. I just tasted it for the first time. I was spending the night at my friend Tiffany's house and she showed me her mom's bottle of vodka.

"Taste some," she smiled, before taking a swig herself. So I did. It burned all the way down my throat and seemed to come out my ears. "Why do grown-ups drink this?" I asked, before we went back to prank calling boys. I really never thought about alcohol again, assuming it all tasted terrible, until I was in high school.

My next bout with alcohol came my freshman year of high school. It was actually the summer after; I was spending a lot of time at my friend Laurie's, who lived by the lake in our town. At night, a bunch of guys in her neighborhood always had bonfires and set up tents to drink in, and we started going down there. All they had was beer. I obviously hadn't had much experience with alcohol, but I was about to be a sophomore in high school, and it was becoming the norm for my friends to have some beer if we "went out."

So I took the cold, wet Budweiser can that Laurie's neighbor, Paul, handed me and attempted to open it as if I'd been cracking the babies open for years. It became apparent that wasn't true when, with my 100-pound frame and zero tolerance, I was feeling the effects after managing to swallow down most of the can. Even though I thought the taste was vile, I loved how it made me feel. I had always had a crush on Paul, but was never comfortable enough around boys to really talk to him. Beer, however, gave me a different personality. Instead of being uptight and shy, I was suddenly giggly and flirtatious. Paul seemed to like this new Sara, too. This was the beginning of my love affair with alcohol.

Alcohol wasn't a big part of the rest of my high school career. I indulged in it whenever I was at parties, or we went to school dances –

basically whenever it was there and all my friends were doing it. And again, as with my first experience with it, it always gave me confidence with boys, confidence I definitely didn't have otherwise. Most of the time I drank Zima or Bartles & James wine coolers. I know. Don't judge me; I didn't know any better. Plus, that was what the guys who were of age always seemed to buy for us. I have to say, they were on to something. While I'd manage to suck beer down despite the taste, I found Zima and wine coolers to be pretty yummy. So of course, all the girls drank more that way.

It wasn't until my senior year of high school that alcohol became a more permanent fixture. We were all close to going off to college, where booze would become a staple, so we had to practice. I had started dating Ben, who, as it turned out later, was pretty much an alcoholic. I met him at the drive-in, though I'd run into him once before that. Neither of us had really spoken that time, though. It was on a dimly lit street, walking home from a festival. He and his friends ran into my group of friends. I saw him, and all I knew was I was in love. He was the cutest boy I'd ever seen. And he seemed somewhat interested in me.

The night at the drive-in is somewhat blurry, because I'd had a lot to drink. (That's what we did in high school. Go to the drive-in, park in the back row, get drunk, and mingle.) So Ben's friends and my friends arranged a little mingling session for Ben and me. I remember sitting on the bed of the truck with him, making awkward conversation. Feeling giddy out of my mind because I wanted to be with him. I breathed in his enticing cologne and politely complimented the tattoo on his leg. I tried to hold it together, to not let my feelings show yet. It seemed too good to be true for me; he was perfect. At least at that point in time he was.

Ben and I started spending more and more time together, mostly with our friends. Even though I was fine without it, he started packing wine coolers for me whenever we did anything, wherever we went. A bunch of us went to a haunted woods around Halloween, and he opened the trunk of the car to reveal the ammunition.

"I'm not drinking!" I exclaimed, wondering who this guy was I'd chosen to date.

"Oh. Okay," shrugged Ben, closing the trunk as he took a swig of his Natural Light. A few weeks later for our homecoming dance, however, I totally drank the wine coolers he'd bought me. After all, it was a dance. And it gave me the confidence to kiss him without him having to make the first move for once. I liked buzzed Sara.

Of course, this was the year I also gave birth to "cheating Sara" - a Sara I've never liked. While alcohol definitely made me more open and talkative, it also seemed to sometimes blur the line between what is simply "talking" to another guy and what is "ferociously making out in a hot tub" with another guy. Yeah.

My parents were gone, so naturally, I had a party at our house. At the time, I worked at a CD store in town. A guy I worked with in his 20s, Ron, was supposed to stop by with our alcohol. Once he did, he stayed and proceeded to get drunk with us. Ben was out of town. At first I was resistant to Ron's advances. Didn't he know I had a boyfriend? The next thing I knew, I was in my parents' hot tub in my bra and underwear, listening to Ron marvel at what "firm breasts" I had. (I was 17, so of course they were. May they rest in peace.) I didn't even realize what I'd done until long after, when I was sobering up. What did I do?

I felt completely awful when the reality of the situation hit me, and I did end up telling Ben, because I hadn't wanted or intended on anything happening. If only I had stopped drinking in high school…perhaps nothing like that would have happened again.

The End of Ben

I don't believe in happy endings. ~ Jeanette Winterson

Toward the end of my senior year of high school, I started pulling away from Ben, assuming we'd attend different colleges in the fall and automatically break up. This was never discussed; I just had heard about enough different high school couples to understand that this is what happens.

Ben started to catch on one day when he was leaving my parents' house and I was being especially distant. He inquired about it, and I said, "Well...I just figured before fall we'd break up...right?" He started laughing at me, telling me I was funny and crazy and that's not at all what he'd planned on.

"Oh..." I responded, confused, and partly relieved and flattered that he still wanted to be with me. This whole thing completely changed my expectations of the future, however, and I wasn't sure how to process it or where to go from there. How would that work, with us at different schools, and all the new opportunities we'd have?

Well, the way it worked was, Ben decided to go to the college I chose to go to. I wasn't as thrilled as one might imagine I'd be. Maybe because deep down I knew we were doomed, and us at the same school only guaranteed my possible run-ins with an ex-boyfriend for the next four years or so.

I remember the day my parents dropped me off at school for freshman orientation. There were so many students and so many unknowns, and I'm a highly wound, anxious person who hates the unknown, so I was a nervous wreck. I didn't have all the books I needed for classes yet, and this bothered me tremendously. I wanted to have each and every one of those books in my possession before my parents left that day.

We scrambled from bookstore to bookstore in vain to locate every text and course pack so I could breathe. My parents kept trying to get me to relax. Ben kind of hung out on the lawn with another guy who'd come to college with him from high school. Ben's parents hadn't stayed at all, and I was so caught up in my own perfectionism and making sure I was ready to excel in college that I didn't take the time to try and be with him when he probably needed it. But then again, in high school and the beginning of college, I wasn't exactly an open and vulnerable girlfriend. I was shy and insecure.

So after I got done bawling when my parents left (yes, I did - like a baby), leaving me to fend for myself among the thousands of nameless freshmen faces, I tried to settle in to my new role of college student. My dad had filled out my rooming form, and he'd of course chosen me to stay in the honors dorm. Ben's dorm was all the way across campus. My dorm was mostly filled with diligent students who kept their doors shut, and when they did emerge, they looked as if they quite possibly had never seen the sun. Pale. Blinding me pale.

My roommate was a sorority girl, who, at first, seemed to mesh with me okay. We both liked to go out and party; we were a few of the residents of the honors dorm who seemed to enjoy a social life. Heidi, my roommate, had a boyfriend who played baseball at another college, who also happened to be a giant dumbass. The first time I met him he said, "Hey, you guys'll have to let me know when you start having your periods at the same time. That's supposed to happen when girls live together." I stared at him, while Heidi rolled her eyes and grabbed his arm, dragging him to the other room.

"Other room," by the way, refers to the shoe box sized area our bunk beds were in. The adjoining room had two desks, a mini fridge, and an inflatable couch. Yes. We had an inflatable couch. And a chair. It was like passing out on a raft.

The first week of school there were tons of parties. All of the fraternity houses were within walking distance of our dorm (well, technically, everything was, since I didn't have a car on campus) and we'd usually pre-drink in our dorm, which was against the rules, so we had to sneak around. Heidi's boyfriend usually provided it, and if he didn't, there was one liquor store that was known for selling to anyone.

Once we got a good buzz, my roommate and a couple of her friends and I usually started walking to the parties. I saw Ben at the first party we went to, and it was weird. I think we were both realizing at that point that this was definitely not high school. We didn't have the communication skills necessary to prolong a relationship. I saw him from across the room, and it was like I didn't exist. He'd been spending time at a frat house whose members were known for being assholes, and I could tell he was definitely becoming one. At least around the "brothers." He drank a lot in high school, but he started drinking a lot more as soon as we got to college. Every party we'd go to, he'd end up in a fight. He was a belligerent drunk. I didn't have a strong enough impetus to break up with him yet.

Well, after I'd been to my share of college parties and spent enough time in classes, I started realizing there were other guys in the world paying attention to me, guys who might not be belligerent, drunken assholes. So I told Ben I wanted to talk.

He came over to my dorm one night, and I more or less explained that I cared about him, but I thought we should cool it and both just figure out what we wanted. He said, "So…you want to be friends?"

"Yeah. I guess," I said.

He left. And that was that. Only that wasn't that. Like any unhealthy relationship should, this one continued far after I knew it shouldn't. This was partly my fault. Ben would call me, or I would get drunk and call Ben. I wanted to move on; I did. But at the end of the day, I was alone at school, and he was familiar. Plus, as he'd stated, we were friends, right?

Then came the turning point.

I went out one night with some friends I'd met at my new job, an eatery on campus. We pre-drank in my dorm. Bacardi 151. Mistake number one of the night. And this was a girl who got drunk regularly on Boone's Farm. I obviously didn't understand what the "151" meant, as I generally didn't drink liquor. Ever. We played a few drinking games in the room until I was nice and wasted. I don't remember the walk to the party. This would be my first-ever blackout.

I remember the party was dark. And loud. And crowded. I know I immediately got separated from my friends, and I remember making out with a guy I'd just met - and right in the middle of the party, up against the wall. I couldn't tell you his name or what he looked like.

I remember my friends carrying me out of the party.

I remember being back in my dorm room. My answering machine was flashing. I played the message, and it was Ben. I didn't know what time he'd called, but he said, "Hey, this is Ben.   Just seeing what you're up to. I'll be up 'til the ass-crack of dawn so give me a call if you want."

I was blitzed out of my mind, so I don't remember what I said when I called him, but he came over. I know we started making out in my dorm room, and then we were on the floor in the hallway. I can only assume because I'd fallen there. The vivid memories from this night are mixed in with blacked-out periods, so all I have are the parts in which I wasn't blacked out. But those parts are clearer than almost any other time of my life.

When we were on the floor, he suddenly got angry. "I'm tired of you only wanting me when you're drunk," he said.

The next part I remember is when we were in his dorm room. I don't remember the walk there. We were on his bed, which was the top bunk. I was starting to pass out. I remember lying there, paralyzed, suddenly aware of everything going on around me, but I couldn't open my eyes. I couldn't articulate. He suddenly wasn't beside me. I heard him on the floor below, and the sound of shattering glass. Then he started screaming, "I cut myself! I cut myself!" I didn't know what was going on. Was I dreaming?

The next thing I knew, he was on top of me. There are so many drunken moments that I will never know the true details of, and then there are those moments so chilling and traumatizing that they immediately sobered me up. I will never forget this, as long as I live. I was lying there with his body on top of me, hovering over me. Then I heard him say, "Maybe you'll be sorry when you wake up and see my blood on you, bitch." I could feel something dripping on my neck. I wanted to scream. I wanted to cry. But I couldn't. Nothing would come out. I think I went into shock.

He had my pants down then and was trying to have sex with me. I wanted to tell him to stop, that it wouldn't work anyway, (TMI: I had a tampon in), but he must've realized it at that point because he stopped and then was trying to enter my mouth. That's when, for whatever reason, I snapped out of it. I sprang to life, pushing him off of me, pulling my pants up in the process. I jumped down off the bed and sprinted out of the room. I ran all the way from his dorm back to mine. I had never run so fast in my life. It felt like my life depended on it. It was snowing. Hard. It was actually beautiful, had I not been trapped in my own personal horror movie. I kept looking behind me as I ran, huffing and puffing, yet barely breathing. When I was almost to the dorm, I looked, and he was behind me, running after me. He stopped, though, when I got to the entrance. We both stared at each other for second. I'm not sure what I saw in his eyes. Regret? Sorrow? I don't know.

I was still so drunk yet sober enough to know that this was the most hurtful thing that had ever happened to me. I turned away from him and went inside the dorm. Luckily, he couldn't get in. It was locked and I'd have to buzz him.

The second I got to my room I called my mom, explaining what happened between choked sobs. I looked in the mirror and didn't see blood, and then started wondering if I'd imagined it all. Or maybe I was hoping I'd imagined it all. My mom told me to tell my RA, so I woke her up. By then it was 5 a.m. She groggily told me to try and get some sleep and let her know if he bothered me again and that we would talk later.

I went to sleep, only to have bad dreams. When I woke up in the afternoon, it took a second for everything to sink in. I was so confused. Had that really happened? Maybe I'd imagined it.

On our way to the eatery that night, I told a few close friends what had happened. Ben worked in the eatery, and I prayed to God that he wouldn't be there. My friends tried to reassure me and told me they'd be there for me if anything happened. I didn't want to see him again. Ever.

We walked into the building, and there he was, across the room, behind a cash register. His arm was completely wrapped up, like in a cast. My heart sank. So I hadn't imagined it. I was a wreck at the realization, although my sanity was intact. At least I hadn't hallucinated.

He stared at me from across the room; as soon as our eyes locked, it was a mixture of sadness and fear, maybe. I didn't know. I didn't know anything anymore.

It took months and months - maybe years - to get over him. He was my first love. My first everything. The boy who used to climb into my bedroom window at night. The boy who wrote me stacks and stacks of love letters. Some of them made me cry, they were so moving. The boy who stole my heart. I couldn't believe someone I'd loved and trusted could say those awful things to me, do those awful things to me. What had any of our time together meant? Who was he?

I went to my first counselor after that, though it didn't help. She was basically an intern on campus. She didn't provide me with any tools to help with my feelings, help with the dark depression I was in. So I found my own tools. I drank a lot. I couldn't eat, but I could drink. And smoke. A lot. I cried. A lot. I cried in the shower. Sobbed. Sobbed and let my tears fall as they blended with the water shooting out of the faucet. I listened to sad songs. I *Watched Breakfast at Tiffany's*, hoping that it would heal me, "Moon River" would heal me, Audrey Hepburn would heal me. Nothing worked.

I still don't know what happened that night, I mean, why he did that. He'd cut himself on a glass mug, I'd learned later, and I think it was an accident. Fine. But the rest of what he did was no accident.

I think I'm "over it" now, but maybe enough time has gone by that I don't think about it too much. Or maybe it's something you don't ever really "get over." I do know, looking back on that first relationship, that there is a pattern. Every long-term male relationship I entered into after that contained the one similar component of alcohol abuse. Obviously I've had my own issues, but if I wasn't the one with the problem, the guy I was with had the problem. It's always been there. I'm sure I could psychoanalyze for years why it is I seek out men who are like me in that respect.

I've actually seen Ben and talked to him several times since then. We've even talked about that night, and I don't think he understands, either. Although, sadly, I was also too drunk the night we talked about it to really remember the conversation.

Factory Man

There is an optical illusion about every person we meet. ~ *Ralph Waldo Emerson*

Once upon a time, what should have remained a perfect fantasy became an ugly reality. This would be the second alcoholic I fell in love with. Well, I thought it was love at the time.

The summer after I turned 20, I worked in a factory on my break from college. It sucked. I had to be there super early, and even though I lived approximately 30 seconds away from the place, I was chronically late – which means that I was speeding 90 miles an hour and turning into the parking lot on two wheels every day to sprint inside, clock in, and finish putting my shoes on while everyone else was already doing the "warm-up" we were supposed to do before we got on the assembly line.

The job was boring. They had music on all day, so that was something, but other than that, you had to create your own entertainment while working. I usually started conversations with people working next to me, which changed periodically throughout the day. The conversations always inevitably turned sexual, especially when talking to men. There was one man in particular who I'd noticed my first day there – Justin. He was really built, with these intense blue eyes, and he was rugged, a la Javier Bardem. Justin, I decided immediately, was completely out of my league. He seemed quite a bit older, first of all, plus I figured he was married with kids or something. I just liked to look at him.

Toward the end of the day one time, my team leader was assigning jobs to me and another college temp girl to do until it was time to leave. The girl and I had agreed in an earlier conversation that Justin was hot, so when our team leader was saying something about how one of us would be working with Justin for the rest of the day, we both jumped up and down pleading, "Oooooh, pick me!" He ended up picking me.

I nervously and excitedly made my way over to an area toward the back of the factory where Justin was working, hoping I wouldn't come across as a complete dork. I wasn't necessarily accustomed to spending a lot of time with ridiculously good-looking men, and while I knew I was smart, I didn't feel pretty (and certainly not sexy), although I always wanted to be. I'd had one boyfriend at this point and we were both new at everything a relationship encompasses. I wasn't exactly confident or experienced in any way. Justin introduced himself when I approached, and I did my best to appear completely aloof. The conversation consisted of small talk – where I went to college, what I was studying. I found out he wasn't married – well, he technically wasn't divorced yet – separated and getting divorced.

Spending a couple hours with him catapulted my crush-from-a-safe-distance to full-fledged *I want him*. And not even, *I want to have sex with him*. That idea actually terrified me, since I still felt pretty inadequate in that department. It was more like I wanted to be with him. I felt this thing for him. I had never experienced this strong, immediate, animalistic attraction before. Everyone I'd ever liked or been with had been a boy. And this was a man. In my mind, though, it was still a crush. I never once had any notion that anything in reality would manifest of this infatuation. It was like the crush I'd had on my high school biology teacher – something fun but safe that wouldn't or couldn't go anywhere.

Over the next few weeks Justin and I started talking and working together more, and I'd become more comfortable and relaxed, opening up and letting my real personality show. I allowed my sarcasm to take over, which is my safety net. Justin seemed to like it, as he'd shoot a comment right back at me, or laugh at the things I said. Justin and all the other guys at work liked to joke about sex incessantly. He'd yell to one of the other guys on the line, "Hey Tom, you get any head this weekend?" And everyone would laugh and talk about sex for the rest of the hour. Since Justin assumed up to this point that I was quiet, shy, and a "goody-goody" (and by all means, I pretty much was) I decided to show him I wasn't as reserved as he thought. One Monday morning as soon as we started working on the line, I walked by Justin and a few other guys and asked, "Hey Justin, get any head this weekend?" His jaw dropped as I walked away, leaving the other guys to burst into laughter.

That sort of opened the floodgates.

A few of my friends who were also college temps worked with me at the factory, and after work most days we would talk over cigarettes or Coronas (depending on if someone of legal age was with us to provide alcohol). Justin became the focus of our conversations. All my friends knew I had a major crush on him. It was fun to daydream about him, and it gave me something to look forward to in the otherwise dismal, dreary life on the assembly line.

Then one day, when I was home from work, my mom came into my bedroom with a puzzled look, handing me the phone. "It's some guy," she said. "Hello?" I asked hesitantly. "Sara," was the husky reply. "Yes?" I tried to control the butterflies that threatened to leap out of my throat. "This is Justin."

I couldn't believe it.

It was actually happening. He was calling me! I tried to remain calm and pretend like this was completely typical; attractive men old enough to be my father called me all the time. I could hear other people in the background, and right then another guy who worked at the factory, one of Justin's friends, grabbed the phone. "Sara?" I heard.

"Yeah?"

"This is Tom."

"Oh, hi."

"Justin wants you to come over."

"What?"

I heard some background noise before Justin got back on the phone. "Don't listen to him," he said. I'm drinking with Tom and John. They're drunk."

"Oh. Okay." I said.

"You know who you look like?" he asked.

"Who?"

"Pocahontas. We're at John's house, and John's daughter has this Pocahontas bedspread. You look just like her." (For the record, my hair was really long at this time and I'd dyed it black. I also used to maintain a golden brown tan as if it were my job.)

"Oh. What?"

"You have the most beautiful brown eyes."

I was in such a state of disbelief at this point – one, that this was happening – two, that he seemed to be interested in me – and three, that he was calling me with all his friends around like they were in junior high. I tried not to let the last part discourage me.

Things escalated after the phone call. The next day at work he invited me to come over that night and hang out. I told my parents I was seeing a movie with a friend and drove the long, curvy roads to his house, which was actually a big trailer. He offered me a beer when I got there and I nervously accepted. That night we both had a couple of beers and talked about his time in school and college, which he never finished, although he made it clear that he was "no dummy."

I talked about college and my friends. We talked about how many people we'd "been with" sexually – two for me. (The second one didn't really count. The location was kinda cool - we were on the concrete in the pouring rain along the Huron River in Canada. But if it happens in another country, it doesn't count. Same with that time in Tijuana.) After he thought for what seemed like forever, he answered, "Ten." At the time I almost fell over dead. Ten people?! It seemed like the entire population. Now I know, obviously, that it was probably more accurate for him to say

500. And I had thought two made me sound like a slut. Nothing beyond talking happened that first night. And...Um...he showed me VHS clips of his high school football glory days. Hey, hindsight is 20/20.

We continued to talk at work, and other people were starting to catch on. "So what's going on between you and Justin?" Curious women would try to casually pry information out of me. I learned relatively quickly that I wasn't exactly liked by most of the female employees. One of them actually told me, "You're skinny and hot, and Justin likes you. So everyone else hates you." Great. Oh well. I hadn't exactly taken the job to find a new BFF. Then the rumors started. "I heard you're dropping out of school and moving in with Justin." I was flabbergasted. Where was this coming from? Nothing had even happened between us!

I did start going to Justin's house more frequently, and therefore lying to my parents more often. As far as they were concerned, I went to the movies a lot that summer.

And Justin was pure country. Ben had worn only J. Crew and was, by anybody's standards, a "pretty boy." Justin, on the other hand, loved hunting, and as I soon discovered, frog gigging. Now, I had never heard of such a thing, but I participated in it one night under the moonlight. I held the bag while Justin punctured each frog and threw it into the bag. Then I sat on his porch swing, trashed, watching him skin frogs. No, seriously. This was so not me. I wanted to be with him so badly...

I was still very guarded when it came to things like sex - meaning I wasn't having it with him right away, and if I did, I wanted him to get tested first. He was not fond of that idea. I realized what different worlds we lived in one day when he said, "It's weird. I feel like I want to see you all the time and we're not even having sex. I've never had that happen before."

He could always say the most perfect thing to turn me inside out. I was supposed to come over one night and he called me that day.

"Come over," he said.

"When?" I asked innocently.

"Five minutes ago."

A thrill passed through my body, as no boy I'd ever dated had said such things with such force. And he was a force. "I crave you," he said. I was weak in the knees. I couldn't breathe; I thought he was amazing. This is what I'd always known it could be like – chemistry and passion and the way movies and books showed it how it should be. I had read *Wuthering Heights* in a literature class, and he was Heathcliff.

I was so naive. So incredibly, pathetically, tragically naive.

Weeks went by and we continued seeing one another. One weekend I was at his place after we'd gone to a party at his friend's. He drove home and we were parked in his driveway talking. "Sara, I love you," he said.

Suddenly it became too real.

"Um...I...I mean, I don't think I love you," I said.

"I do," he said. I want to marry you. I think we'll be married by next July," he said. It was this July. Something triggered in my brain. "What?" I asked, incredulous. "I'm 20 years old. I'm in college. I've known you a month." He got out of the car and slammed the door. I stayed in the car and watched him carry the beer left from the party into the house.

Then I heard a loud crash. And even louder yelling.

I hesitantly got out of the car and walked in the house to see broken beer bottles everywhere, with beer covering the floor and the walls. He was leaning on the kitchen counter, his arms supporting him, biceps bulging, veins popping, head down. I was scared. "I'm sorry," I said. "I didn't mean..." He didn't look up. I didn't know what else to do so I grabbed the broom beside the refrigerator and started sweeping up the messy, wet, broken bottle fragments. He didn't move the whole time. When I was done sweeping, he looked up and I could see he was crying. He hugged me and didn't let go. I was still a little afraid of him at this point, afraid of what would happen if I let go. So I didn't.

The next day he didn't remember any of it.

While that drunken, violent night was a red flag for me, I figured he was going through a rough time with the impending divorce and tried to cut him some slack. It was around this time that I'd clued my parents in on what was going on – that there was a guy I really liked who I was seeing who was quite a bit older than I. That didn't go over well.

Justin met my parents once – he picked me up one time for an actual "date," as opposed to getting drunk and sitting around the fire pit listening to John Mellencamp or Bob Seger at his place - even if he did say the girl in "Night Moves" reminded him of me - as touching as that was. While both of my parents shook his hand, neither one smiled, and through clenched teeth they failed to disguise their displeasure. I thought his eyes had looked bloodshot when he came to pick me up, and he told me later that he'd had a case of beer before coming over because he was nervous to meet my parents. Red flag number two. Of course I dismissed it, thinking his tolerance was so high, a case to him was like half a beer to me.

It wasn't much longer before he grew increasingly distant. He was acting...different. Like he wanted nothing to do with me all of a sudden. He started blowing me off, so I backed off, thinking he was preoccupied with getting divorced. I didn't want to seem needy and drive him completely away.

Then one day I was working next to Justin on the assembly line. He was distant and reticent. It was almost time to go home...and then a woman came up and started talking to Justin. I felt jealous immediately. I listened to their conversation carefully. I studied the body language. I knew this was more than a friendship.

Shortly after, I found out from someone at work that he was cheating on me with his ex-girlfriend, someone he'd cheated on his wife with. And someone who gave him sex – something I didn't. I was devastated the day I found out. I came home from work and ate an entire large pizza. I then locked myself in my bedroom, curling into the fetal position on my bed. I sobbed myself to sleep.

\I beat myself up for months that I had been so stupid, so gullible, so ridiculous to think someone like him would be interested in me – I should have known better. After a few years I realized I was way too good for him – not because he lived in a trailer or worked in a factory – not at all – but because he was a selfish, mean, inconsiderate person. A piece of my innocence was stripped away the day I found out he hadn't cared about me at all, and it was replaced by something jaded, cynical, and broken. The idea of that still makes me sad.

The Bodybuilder

Everything will line up perfectly when knowing and living the truth becomes more important than looking good. ~ Alan Cohen

Josh and I met the summer I was twenty-one, home from college until fall classes resumed. It was the night of my mom's birthday party. My dad, brother, our immediate relatives, and her closest friends held a big surprise party for her in a hall in my hometown. My friend Stephanie and I had plans to go out afterward. Looking good, as it was summer, we spent every second of the day lying in the sun, ingesting little more than cigarettes and Diet Mountain Dew. We were both tan and skinny. (I didn't say healthy.)

So right after the party we drove to a bar the next town over. We were both single and ready to mingle! Also…I had had my first one-night-stand the night before. It was the brother of some guy who Stephanie was kind of seeing. I have no idea why I did it. Stephanie was shocked. That wasn't me.

But it was becoming me. As soon as I had that one-night-stand, I adopted the attitude of, well, I've already had one; I've catapulted myself from good girl to bad girl, so why not keep going? I'd "broken the seal." I was already "ruined." (Much of my early twenties were spent doing very important things like drinking until blacking out and/or getting naked with a stranger.)

Stephanie and I got to the bar and started dancing, when she nudged me, "Look over there!" The most muscular arms I had ever seen in person, attached to a smokin' hot body and attractive face was in my direct line of vision. "He's hot," I said in awe to Stephanie, wiping the drool from my chin.

Hope was immediately abandoned, as I would never gain the interest of a human being that impossibly good-looking. Somehow, though, he and his friend made his way to us and seemed to actually be interested. And the hot one, Josh, was interested in me! He started making small talk and I obliged but never put much stock into it, figuring he was merely being nice.

I went to the bathroom, and a girl I'd seen with Josh earlier said, "Josh wondered where you went! He really likes you!" Disbelief doesn't even begin to describe it. I turned to stare at myself in the grungy bathroom mirror, looking hard to try and see what he saw.

Me?

When I exited the bathroom, the bar was closing down and he was waiting for me. "So can I get your number and we can get something rolling?" he asked. It seemed too good to be true.

Well, it was true. Josh and I began dating and I was on top of the world. He was by far the hottest guy I'd ever seen, and I was still in shock that he'd find me attractive. (I was fine until sixth grade. That's when I began the fun journey of bad perms, pimples, and braces. People made fun of me. Hence my low self-esteem.) However, men were starting to appear interested in me. I'd "blossomed" since high school, which means I went from a B to D-cup. My hair had also grown out, which apparently can make a world of difference for men (although as it turns out, the focus inevitably becomes the vagina, which they prefer without hair. Go figure.)

With Josh, the signs were subtle at first. We were on a date and he asked me if there were one thing I could change about his body, what would it be? Laughing, because his body was ripped to perfection, I giggled out a "Nothing!" Assuming he'd say the same, I asked him. "You could work on your arms," he said with a semi-disgusted smirk. My heart sank and I felt a lump grow in my throat followed by a little anger, but I rationalized to myself and calmed down a little. Well, yeah, I guess I could work on my arms, right? What's so wrong with that?

Josh and I started working out regularly together, and he pushed me through workouts, harder and harder with each one while he simultaneously powered through his own gym routine, sweat dripping from his blue bandana. Jaw clenched, veins popping, he grunted angrily with every bicep curl, lat pull-down, or squat that he performed, stopping now and then to guzzle water from a gallon jug and shoot me a casual thumbs –up. I hadn't really seen him proud or impressed until we hit the gym together. His eyes would widen and he'd smile, congratulating me every time I completed a difficult set.

The positive reaction I got was what drove my addiction to please him, and my addiction to attain bodily perfection. He began to increasingly compliment me - the more muscle I gained and fat I lost. And I thrived on it. While he had never seemed too fazed by the fact that I was working toward a Master's degree in literature and had a lot of smart things to say, he was thrilled to notice that my ass was firming up.

Josh, who appeared to have other interests when we first met, like golf and Jim Carrey movies, slowly was revealing himself to be more and more superficial. I figured the problem lay in me. Maybe I was too judgmental. Having a great body is no small feat, right? Deep thoughts are overrated, I told myself. Aren't we all superficial on some level? Clothes and makeup meant a lot to me; maybe Josh and I were more alike than I thought. Maybe it was me. Besides, how could someone so hot and phenomenal in bed be wrong for me?

My exercising spiraled out of control and my now fervent desire to emulate a cover girl on *Women's Fitness* caused me to stop eating altogether, and when I did eat, I got rid of it most of the time. Josh was so proud of me at this point and loved to show me off like a shiny new car. He hadn't stopped offering his "constructive criticism," however, with helpful tips like, "You know if you get your waist smaller your boobs will look even bigger," and "If I were rich I'd take care of that bump on your nose." He also freely distributed his fashion advice, which means he preferred that I dress like a stripper, and I politely accommodated.

My friends were growing less and less fond of him and tried to at first tactfully, and then not so tactfully, tell me we weren't right for each other, but by then I had invested so much time on the relationship and money on a gym membership that it seemed like a waste to give up now.

I became obsessed with pleasing him.

Although I had smoked when we met, I gave it up for him (even though he chewed, but that was okay for some reason). Smoking behind his back one night and his discovery of this led to him going ballistic, screaming in my face and becoming unacceptably aggressive. Somehow I always turned it on myself, explaining away his anger and rationalizing that he's right; smoking isn't healthy.

So many times during the course of our relationship, as my identity slipped further and further away, I told myself I was actually becoming a better person with Josh in my life – after all, my body had never looked better. Plus, he really was trying. Even though he didn't manage to get flowers sent on Valentine's Day, it wasn't his fault. All the florists were booked. He even watched *Sex and the City* with me one night.

On the downside, it really bothered me and made me feel insecure when he made remarks about the way other women looked, but I didn't let him know. I became everything he'd ever wanted, down to my perfectly manicured fingernails which I'd always bitten away at before, but he'd found that "horrible." My hair was cut the way he wanted. I was his Pygmalion. Had he gotten the reference, I would have told him this, but I'm pretty sure that's not explained in *MuscleMag*.

When I went back to college he visited me on the weekends, bringing duffel bags full of supplements and cases of tuna. I can't forget carrying cooked chicken breast in my purse if we did go out, so he could eat his protein around the clock. I accepted this, and when people in the clubs gave me sideways glances, some even asking me, "What the hell is that?"

"Just my boyfriend's grilled chicken breast," I would answer nonchalantly.

One time we were at my apartment after going out drinking. He brought up the topic of sexual fantasies. Of course I'd had them, but I'd never shared them. Plus I'd never thought about anyone else when I was having sex with my boyfriend. Well, apparently, he had. He proceeded to describe thoughts of silicone-enhanced celebrities. The fantasy conversation made me want to kill myself. Instead, I figured I needed to be more of a freak in the sack to fulfill all of his fantasies myself. So I did whatever he wanted.

When we weren't going out drinking, we'd spend nights renting movies which we never got through because we always had sex. Sometimes it would start out playfully, sort of like a wrestling match. Being the smaller, less muscular of us, I'd do my best to fight back, because sometimes he didn't know his own strength. One time to make him stop pinning me down, I grabbed at his chest. He got in my face with an expression full of rage and screamed, "Don't you ever grab my pec again!" Immediately I started crying and he eventually apologized...but left while I was still in tears.

We'd gone out somewhere close to his house once. I was crying. I don't even know why. Whenever I'd reach my highest level of intoxication, I'd always cry. Always. We walked home from the bar to his house, and I didn't want to go inside. I didn't want his parents to see me like this, drunk and crying. He kept insisting that I go in, and I didn't want to. He was getting mad about it. He went in and I stayed outside for a while, trying to get myself together.

When I got in the house, it was mostly dark. Everyone had gone to bed. I made my way into the living room and sat on the couch where Josh was sitting. *The Tonight Show* was on TV. "Are you sorry?" he asked me.

I sat there silently for a second, thinking this whole situation was surreal. I was still drunk. I wasn't sure where this was going, and I didn't think I was in the wrong, but I acquiesced. Somehow I always rationalized that he was right. I said I was sorry. Before I knew it he was undressing me and on top of me, making me say over and over again how sorry I was while he railed me hard with everything he had. "Now are you sorry?" he kept saying. On the outside I went along with it, but on the inside I was dying, sinking, drowning. This didn't feel right at all, and the realization of what was happening was breaking me. Once it was over he said he was tired and wanted to go to bed, as if nothing had happened. So I told myself the same thing.

Even though a voice in the back of my head was whispering on a regular basis by this point that this wasn't right, this wasn't healthy, this wasn't me, I told the voice to shut up.

He visited me at college one weekend in January and we went to a small party one night at a friends' house. There was six feet of snow on the ground at this time. Once we trudged through the snow to get to the party, Josh and I snuck off to the bathroom, something not unusual for us, since, looking back, sex was the only thing that kept us together.

We started making out and it got pretty heated. Something changed. He started banging my head against the hard tile bathroom floor. All I can remember is digging my fingernails as hard as I could into his arms so he'd stop. He finally did. To yell at me.

He ran out of the bathroom screaming that he's done with me; he's done with my parties, done with my friends, done with everything. He didn't explain further and I don't know what his motivation was but it didn't matter. The ten or so people in the room who had been immersed in the party, laughing, drinking, and listening to music, immediately became somber deer in headlights, their eyes darting from Josh to me and back again, wondering what the hell was going on. How did I feel at this point? Numb. Frozen. Paralyzed. My first instinct was to sprint out of the house and not look back. So I did. In my thigh-high boots, skirt, and tank top, I ran and ran the best I could through the shoveled path between the six feet of snow.

When I looked back, he was nowhere to be seen. I was a bundle of fear, hurt, and sadness – packaged in a leather mini and sparkly tank. A car full of guys pulled up and asked if I needed a ride so I got in. My address somehow escaped my lips and I luckily got dropped off without being gang-banged. As soon as I reached my apartment I called my friend Joe, sobbing about what had happened. Joe said he was on his way over, but Josh got there first. Somehow he turned the whole thing on me once again; I had angered him to the point of violence. And I believed him.

He said he was leaving. He started packing his belongings into his black duffle bag, all the while maintaining this agitated demeanor, as if, once again, this was my fault. And of course, again, I told myself that this was my fault. Apologizing through my sobs, I begged him not to leave. After all, he was so angry and upset with me, and I had caused it. It was simply a big misunderstanding triggered by drinking. 'This wasn't like him,' I thought, something I'd thought many times.

The next morning he was sorry, and although I was hesitant, I figured I should blame it on the alcohol. This sort of thing happened more than once, which led to my breaking up with him more than once. Yet we kept getting back together. I couldn't live with or without him.

The funny thing is, the realization that my identity was gone and I abhorred the thread of me I had left – the me I was with him – didn't hit me when it should have – it came out of the sky one day when I wasn't even with Josh; I was alone. I was aimlessly flipping through a magazine, when something struck me like cognitive lightning. 'Who am I?' I wondered. 'When is the last time I did something I enjoy doing? What *do* I enjoy doing?' This wave of truth washed over me; I felt my whole body come to a conclusion. Did I know who I was anymore? Not at all. Being myself, doing the things that fulfilled me, engaging in activities that brought me peace, following paths that agreed with my sensibilities – where…where did that go?

I missed me.

It wasn't a quick, painless process. The break-up dragged on and on, complete with those post-break-up drunk dials (cue Lady Antebellum's "Need You Now") and sex I regretted every time. There were days I could not physically get out of bed. Kleenex made a killing off of me.

Logically it made no sense – I was leaving something unhealthy, something damaging. I think heartbreak followed because of everything I had put into it and I had wanted it to work so badly. Even though all along I had really known he wasn't the one for me, I had wanted him to be the one. The reality that he wasn't, that he never would be, left a giant aching hole in my heart because I had known this but had refused to accept it. There was sadness, intense sadness. The sadness wasn't necessarily because he was gone, though. The sadness was because I had been gone for so long.

I still have trouble setting foot in a gym.

My Least Favorite Mistake

Good judgment comes from experience, and experience comes from bad judgment. ~ *Rita Mae Brown*

It was over ten years ago. I remember when I first felt the spark with Alan. I was at his house, on my way to work out, and Jenny, his wife, was telling me a story about her and her boyfriend, this guy she'd been having an affair with. I hadn't known her very long, maybe a month (we met as bartenders working at the same bar) and we clicked instantly. Party girls can spot fellow party girls from a mile away. We worked together for the first time at the bar and she asked me, "Do you drink on the job?"

"Hell yes, I drink on the job!" I said. And the rest is history.

We both drank the entire night on nights when we worked together, and we had a blast. We cranked up the music, flirted with every attractive male customer, said crazy and outrageous things. It was fun. I had learned that she had kids and that she was married. It didn't take too much time or too many tequila shots; however, for her to open up to me that she was having an affair. I was still with Josh, my bad-for-my-self-esteem boyfriend, and she kept emphasizing to me that I should end the relationship now and explore my options before I got married so I wouldn't regret it. So that's when I broke up with Josh. To get over him, I had sex with other men. A lot.

It wasn't very long before one of those men was Jenny's husband.

I want to make one thing clear. I am not exactly a home wrecker. I knew she was cheating on him. Does it make what I did right? Not at all. It's still wrong. I'll own up to that. But I did not barge into a happy marriage and swoop her husband out from under her while she was home knitting every night. I feel bad about what happened and I always will. I've made a lot of stupid decisions, especially in my 20s, and Alan occupied about three years' worth of bad decisions. But everything that's happened has contributed to putting me where I am right now, and where I am right now is where I'm supposed to be.

I had broken up with Josh but hadn't completely stopped seeing him. And there were many guys coming and going throughout my "relationship" with Alan. I didn't care about myself at all then, which really only became apparent to me when I could look back on it.

One thing remained constant, though, and that is that I was drunk. I was always drunk. Drunk, hungover, drunk, hungover, drunk, hungover. It was the pattern of my existence. It started to seem really normal. That, and getting regular STD tests done.

I remember one time specifically when I was getting tested, the woman at the clinic, a nice, soft-spoken, gray-haired lady, asked me how many sexual partners I'd had. When I told her the number, after hesitating a moment (and thinking about it a while, honestly) she stared at me a second, before a concerned look crossed her face and she asked, "Why? You're so pretty." I looked at the floor a while and then looked up with tears in my eyes. "I don't know." That's all I could say.

I engaged in reckless, fatalistic behavior because I didn't care about myself. Didn't care what happened to me. I remember walking across the parking lot one day after teaching an English class (I began teaching at some community colleges shortly after breaking up with Josh) and wishing I'd be diagnosed with something deadly – wishing that something really bad would happen - to justify the completely miserable way I felt all the time. I didn't have a plan to kill myself or anything, but I also didn't care what happened to me. I was severely depressed constantly. I had no real "reason" to feel this way, I thought, which made it harder. The emptiness I felt was swallowing me whole. I was filling the aching, longing void in my heart with alcohol and sex. At the end of the day, I felt a thousand times worse and had a thousand regrets, instead of feeling better, like I wanted.

I'd stopped at Jenny's one day while running errands. Alan had just gotten home from spending the night at a friend's, and he was playing with his kids, who were climbing all over him, giggling and smiling. I had a couple of different reactions to this. First, I was not a fan of kids. I'd never wanted them. But these kids, I liked. I'm not sure why, but they were the first kids I was actually fond of. Secondly, I had never envisioned myself getting married. I mean, once in a while, it crossed my mind, but mostly I couldn't see it. For some reason, as soon as I met Alan, I thought he was exactly the kind of man I'd like to marry. He was cute and hot at the same time, he was a teacher...this fleeting thought passed through my mind, of us sitting in our perfect kitchen one day, drinking coffee and reading the morning paper. He smiled at me and I melted. He was incredibly charming. We made small talk while Jenny was on the phone (with her boyfriend) and when I was leaving, he said, "Hey. Come back anytime," with a smile that had more behind it than I realized at the time. And even though I couldn't see it, I could feel him staring at my ass as I left the room. There was something a little *too* flirty about him.

At the door, I asked Jenny what was wrong with her, cheating on a man like that. She said, "I know, I know! I don't know what to do."

"Jen, he's great! Look at how he is with the kids! And he's hot!"

"I know. I need to figure this out."

I didn't see either of them again until the next weekend, when they both came with a bunch of other friends to our town's festival. The night that changed everything.

We were all in the beer tent and I was feeling pretty good. I decided I wanted to ride one of the festival's rides. No one would go with me. Then Alan volunteered, "I'll go!"

"Oh, okay!" I said, and I found myself surprised, yet delighted. Everyone laughed at us and told us to be good, as we made our way out of the beer tent toward the rides. Alan grabbed my hand to hold it as soon as we were away from everyone, which I liked, but which scared me a little. What does that mean? I wondered, my head spinning a million different ways. I figured he was being goofy and must be a touchy-feely guy in general. The further we got from the crowd, the chattier he got. He looked me up and down, from my high heel wedges to my jean skirt to my cropped pale yellow top. "You're so hot," he said. "All my friends want to fuck you," he said emphatically, and I didn't know whether to feel good about that or disgusted that that's what they'd been talking about when I glanced across the beer tent earlier as he and his friends smiled and waved.

"What?"

"You're just so hot!" he said, and squeezed my hand. I didn't know if he was pretty buzzed, if he talked this way with everyone...I didn't know how all of this should make me feel.

We got up to the rides and learned that they were all shutting down. Since we were all the way over there, Alan said he had to go to the ATM. So we walked across the street. I waited while he got money out, and once he got his money, he grabbed my hand again and we were on our way back. All of a sudden, he yanked me into an alley and started kissing me. Really kissing me. Like his life depended on it. "Oh, Sara..." he breathed between kisses.

I tried to stop him at first. Being the voice of reason, and the voice of what-the-hell-is-going-on, I couldn't let this happen. Only I stopped resisting him and did let it go on a little. Maybe I was caught up in the moment. Maybe I was so attracted to him that it overtook my morals and clouded my judgment for a second. I don't know. I did stop him when he started reaching inside my skirt, telling me he wanted me. I wasn't about to have intercourse with him in the dirty alley next to the ATM. "No, Alan," I said. "We can't."

So we started walking back toward the beer tent, and he didn't seem remorseful, but maybe reflective. "My wife hasn't had sex with me in six months," he said.

"Wow." I had no clue what to say or how to say it. I was still trying to process what had happened. It did explain a lot, though. He asked me if he turned me on, and I said yes, even though I wanted to say no. I knew this was only headed for trouble. The trouble with that was, I was already on that road.

By the time we got back to everyone at the beer tent, they were wondering where we'd been, making jokes that I must've been giving him a blow job on the ride. I laughed nervously and tried not to seem completely transparent.

The next afternoon I was doing some shopping in town when my car stalled. No one was there when I called was home, so I called Jenny. It was super hot out, so I was sitting in my car in the parking lot with my car door open, one leg dangling out the side, trying not to sweat to death as I attempted to get the thing to start again. I told her about my car and where I was.

"Do you want Alan to come jump you?"

The wording alone. Considering the night before...it took everything I had not to laugh/cry/scream at the absurdity of it. Did I want Alan to come jump me?

I could hear Alan in the background, volunteering to come jump me. "Ummm, no! No! I'll be okay. I'll figure it out. I'll get help from someone. I'll be okay; he doesn't have to come all the way over here."

"Are you sure?" Jenny asked. "He can do it."

I heard him again, in the background. "Um, no...really...let me call someone and I'll call you back."

I saw Alan again that very night when Jenny decided to have people over. She'd made tons of food, and there was enough alcohol to keep us all drunk for a month. At first I was hesitant to go. I had such mixed, confused feelings about him. The devil on my shoulder won out, however. When we got there, he said, "You look good," right away, with definite implications. As much as I wanted to fight my urges with Alan, it was nice to get compliments. Josh and I were pretty much officially over, anyway. So even though I knew better, I ignored my inner voice and went with it.

I started drinking and got really loosened up. All my trepidation about him upon our arrival was gone. We were all dancing around the house to the cranked-up music, getting wasted and acting crazy. For some reason Jenny and I made out. (Does there have to be a reason? I've made out with all of my friends. That's normal, right?) Eventually, everyone wanted Taco Bell. Jenny told me she wanted to call her boyfriend, so she suggested I go with Alan to get the food. He raised his eyebrows at me, and off we went.

As soon as we were a safe distance from the house, he started kissing me. While he was driving. Like, *really* kissing me. I found myself completely won over by him, and I no longer resisted it. Instead of driving to Taco Bell, he drove to a church a little ways from it. He started kissing me more intensely once he parked in the parking lot. Then he told me to get in the back. As unreal and insane as this was, something silenced the protest I was feeling inside, for reasons I don't really even understand to this day. I was buzzed, but I wasn't wasted. Sure, part of me wanted to say no. But I didn't.

I got in the back and he undressed me as much as he needed to, then got on top of me. What happened after that didn't last long. He seemed pretty into it, and I pretended to be, but I wasn't. It made me feel used. Yet I allowed him to do it. I was starting to have feelings for him, though, as much as I didn't want to. It was almost like...something I had to go through. So I went against by better judgment and followed my poor, drunk, misguided heart over my head.

That was the beginning of my three-year affair with Alan.

He didn't know about Jenny's cheating for a long time. I always wondered if deep down he knew, if that's how he justified what he did with me. I'll never know. He knew she was gone all the time. He knew she never had sex with him. I know she didn't know about me and Alan. I know this sounds like a *Jerry Springer* episode. I cringe that this was my life. I'm better than that. Yet...it was my life.

When I ended things with Josh, Alan had made sure I knew it wasn't for him. And it wasn't. I broke up with Josh because meeting Alan made me realize that there were guys out there who were better for me. Guys like Alan. I know I did want to be with him, though, that I did want it to work out somehow, as unrealistic as that seemed.

And Jenny actually encouraged me to hit on her husband, oddly. Even though we were secretive about what we were doing, everyone around could sense our chemistry. Jenny would say things such as, "He likes you! You're both teachers! Go for it, Tiger!" It was like she was so preoccupied with her affair that she didn't care what her husband did. Or maybe it was to alleviate guilt...though it seemed she never had any. While she was telling me to do whatever I wanted with her husband, at the same time, she completely trusted him. She would also say, "I could leave Alan for a weekend at the Playboy Mansion and wouldn't have to worry. He will never even admit that another woman is attractive." Whenever she said things like this, I would shift uncomfortably, clear my throat a lot, and express how lucky she was to have a faithful husband.

I was crazy about Alan. I had butterflies every time I was near him, even at the thought of him. I started picturing our future, started picturing us telling Jenny about how we were together. I thought this was it; this was the man of my dreams. When it got to the point that he wouldn't call for months, I told myself that he had the kids all the time that he was a great dad, that Jenny was always out with her boyfriend, and I had to be understanding. I believed him when I voiced my insecurities about this and he told me there was no one else, just me. I believed him when he started saying things like he couldn't wait to start waking up next to me every day. I clung to every ounce of hope, every teensy promise he'd make.

I became completely wrapped up in him. I stared at the phone constantly, willing it to ring, praying and hoping he'd call. And when he did, I dropped whatever I was doing to be with him. He had this power over me that I couldn't let go of.

I felt like maybe I was falling in love with him. Logically, that made no sense. What did we do besides have sex? I even asked him this, as sometimes the logical side of me (aka the sober side, which wasn't around much) spoke up. The masochistic emotional side of me happened to always win. When I did talk about our future and my doubts, he'd overpower me by rubbing my leg or brushing my hair behind my ear and that's all it took. The next thing I knew, it was over, and I was naked and panting on top of his sweaty chest.

So I put all of my hopes into a man who maybe he didn't care about me at all. To convince myself that he did, I constantly drank to the point that my judgment was clouded enough that sex with him seemed like a good idea. Alcohol allowed me to justify it, to numb the pain, to distort the reality of the situation, that I wasn't a girl worthy of being in a relationship with.

I remember a lot of the music I listened to during that tumultuous time, the periods in which he wouldn't call. Certain songs, even when I hear them now, remind me of it. I'd always liked Joni Mitchell's "Both Sides Now," but the lyrics suddenly struck a severe chord with me, and I couldn't even listen to it without crying. Yet I listened to it a lot, because usually music was the only thing that really stopped me from ending my life.

I definitely identified with the lyrics. I "couldn't let him know," couldn't "give myself away." I didn't want to seem weak, or needy, like I hadn't wanted to seem that way with Josh or Justin. I showed my true colors a time or two, but I usually tried to pretend like I was fine. I was fine being some consolation prize because his wife was cheating on him. I pretended I was fine during the time I was with him, and then I cried when he left.

I know I'd have never started this, never had done any of it had I been sober. I was enduring the worst break-up of my life with Josh, and Alan came along and provided the perfect distraction. Except I also still went to Josh's apartment way too often and had post-break-up sex. I left there feeling meaningless, hopeless, and unfulfilled. Then Alan would call, and I'd feel better. Until he didn't call again for weeks, or months. I wanted to die. Every day. As a way to try and ease the pain, I had sex with practically every man I had a conversation with. I let myself be used by everyone, until there was barely nothing left of me. And what was left I didn't like or respect. It was hard to look in the mirror at all and feel anything except self-loathing.

Alan eventually stopped calling altogether.

Even though Jenny had been carrying on her own affair (which had ended by this point), the guilt about what I'd done with Alan had always eaten me alive. Against the advice of every person who knew about it, I got drunk enough one night and worked up the nerve to tell her. I called her. I told her everything.

She didn't talk to me for months after that. Maybe it was even a year. I didn't blame her, in a way. It was kind of an unusual situation, with her having her own affair, but that is crossing a line. You don't have sex with your friend's husband. That should be on a bumper sticker.

After enough time went by, she called me and wanted to get together. She forgave me. We both realized he wasn't at all the man we'd thought he was, the man we'd both fallen for, despite what she'd done behind his back. For whatever reason, when I'd gotten drunk and called her, telling her the truth about everything, I also mentioned that I'd never had an orgasm with Alan. (Hey, when I tell the truth, I tell the *whole* truth.) I know it might seem crazy...but I never really felt secure with him, secure enough to completely let go.

So when Jenny and I met up to talk, she told me she'd confronted Alan with what I'd told her about our affair. She said he'd denied it at first. Then he started calling me a whore. (As if that changed the story somehow.) It did sting a little. And it showed me however hurtfully, but finally, the kind of person he was, the way he felt about me, and how little what had happened between us meant to him. She told me that once he started yelling in denial about the affair, then calling me names that she screamed at him, "Sara never even had an orgasm with you!"

I think that's my favorite part.

I'm not really sure what kept me holding on for so long with Alan – maybe because he remained enough of a challenge yet gave me hope that there could be more, keeping my interest. Every time I started to feel abandoned or used, he'd call and leave me a really sweet voicemail letting me know how great I was and how he couldn't wait to see me again. I guess I wanted to believe the lies. They kept me going, distracted me from the pain I was feeling from the break-up with Josh. Maybe it would have been too painful to face the truth back then – that I wasn't special to Alan, that I could have been anyone. I wanted to believe him when he said I was special. When he said I was smart. When he said I was funny. It hurt to realize that really, even though I might have been those things, that wasn't the reason he was there.

The bottom line is, if a married man (or woman) ever initiates more than a friendship with you, just say no. Always. It won't end well. (If you have to be drunk every time you're with the person, that should tell you something, too.)

The Decision

Doubt is a pain too lonely to know that faith is his twin brother. ~ *Khalil Gibran*

I never wanted to have kids and never wanted to get married. I didn't want either, but I especially didn't want the kid part. I remember in a college literature course reading *Jane Eyre* and seeing the name "Adele" for the first time, thinking, 'That would be a really great name for a girl, like someone's daughter. Not my daughter, of course, but someone else's daughter.'

I was done with men. I had sworn them off. I needed a break. It was at this precise time, of course, when Jenny was dying for me to meet Andy, this "cute, funny" firefighter. She was determined. Reluctantly, I agreed to meet him.

And dammit, I liked him.

So we started seeing each other. I had been with Andy monogamously for about five months, which was a record for me. That's when I started to get the familiar feeling of discomfort. The suffocation of intimacy was closing in on me and closing in tight. I no longer trusted men. I was the one with the upper hand this time. I wasn't going to allow myself to get hurt anymore. So I didn't open up.

Andy and I had spent Memorial Day weekend together the way most single twenty-somethings our age did, by binge drinking. We'd partied Friday, Saturday, and Sunday night together, and as the days went on, the stronger the urge for my freedom grew. I invited him over on Memorial Day "to talk." When he got to my house, we sat outside on my parents' deck (since I, admittedly, still lived with them) and I proceeded to break up with him through the pounding headache of my hangover while chain-smoking and spouting out straightforward sentiments with the occasional analogy thrown in for good measure ("It's like I'm a ship and I need to sail.") After all, he knew I'd been planning on moving away to Charlotte, North Carolina, with my friend Jordan. It wasn't like he shouldn't have seen this coming. Through it all, he forced a smile, and although I knew it wasn't genuine, I figured it wasn't my problem at that point.

When we stood up and he was getting ready to leave, he handed me something. A pregnancy test. "Here," he said. "Since you were late." We had talked earlier about how my period hadn't come, and he knew it was past the point that it usually came. I was always irregular, so I stared at the E.P.T. he clutched in his hand and kind of shrugged.

"O...kay," I stammered. "I mean, I guess I'll take this." I went into the bathroom while he waited. I really don't remember how many seconds I peed on that stick. I don't remember what I was thinking while I peed. All I know is, I did do that, and then waited for the result. I looked at the little lines on the stick and looked at the illustration on the box. I stayed in the bathroom for a long time. When I slowly emerged, with a mixture of shock and disbelief, I said, "Ummm...I can't really tell...I mean, it's hard to tell..."

Andy took one look at the test and said, "It looks to me like you're pregnant."

The whole room was spinning. The ceiling was coming down, the walls were closing in on me, the pattern in the carpet seemed to spring to life and swirl in a million different directions. I suddenly couldn't breathe. I stared at those damn little lines indicating the life already growing inside me. Andy then tried to make a joke, which I can't remember, but I replied, "Um, can you leave?" I watched him dejectedly walk out the door. Then I curled up on the couch and called my friend Renee.

"I'm pregnant." I started bawling the second I said it out loud. While I don't explicitly recall her exact words, I know they were full of surprise. I couldn't stay home by myself so I decided to go to her house. But first I threw away my cigarettes – you know, in case I decided to "keep it."

My Last Rock Bottom

I couldn't remember how to drive. How to breathe. All I could focus on is wanting desperately for the tears welling in my eyes to not start streaming down my face, wanting desperately to suppress the urge to smoke every single one of those cigarettes I'd thrown away.

Wanting desperately.

I had wanted desperately for a lot of things lately. But not this. Not like this. Not in this context, and not like this.

Why did this happen? How did this happen and *why* did this happen to me?

I hated him. He had done this; he had wanted this. He didn't want me to leave, so he made sure to do something to keep me here.

It wasn't possible. It's not possible. There's no way. No way.

No way I'm pregnant.

When I got to Renee's (who, at the time, lived with Jordan, the friend I was moving with to Charlotte) she came to the door with a face full of sympathy (although I swear there was a little of *Thank Jesus it's you and not me* in there). She hadn't told Jordan yet, so we went upstairs to find him packing for our move. "Hey!" he said loudly, and then, softer, upon seeing my face threatening to crumple, "What's wrong?"

"I'm pregnant," I blurted out, and then immediately burst into tears. His entire face changed as he came over to me. He and Renee were both staring quietly, unsure of what to say in this surreal circumstance. I made a lame joke about not having room for a playpen in our Charlotte apartment and Jordan rubbed my shoulder and half smiled as we made our way down the hall to their computer room to do some Googling.

The days and nights that followed consisted of me crying off and on, slowly telling more trusted friends, and nibbling on Saltines to put my miserable 24-hour nausea at bay. The night I found out, after trashing my Camel Special Lights, I went out and bought a bottle of prenatal vitamins, again, "just in case," and I was convinced the entire time I was in line at Kmart that everyone who passed me could already tell I was with child.

Every night when my parents were safely in bed I went online and learned everything I could about abortion. The questions I kept coming back to were, Will I feel guilty? Will I regret it? I read a lot about those themes and kept telling myself that this thing, this "baby," was a cluster of cells right now; it wasn't really anything, and this was not in my life plans. I called the people I trusted the most. All the ones who had kids said the same thing, "You will regret not having the baby. You will never regret having it." I told them all the same thing, "But I'm different; I'm not you. I can't have this baby; I don't want this baby."

I eventually made an appointment at the nearest abortion clinic. One of my friends took off work to drive me. I called the clinic the morning of and asked all kinds of questions. "Oh, girls come in here, some of them seven or eight times," was one of her answers when I'd asked about the pain. I'd been brushing my hair in the mirror and froze. That floored me; I was having an abortion conversation like we were talking about a pedicure appointment. The woman on the phone said, "If you're at all not sure about this, don't come in. Take some time to think about it." I hung up the phone and stared into the mirror.

Who am I?

The following week I moped around the house, staying in while everyone else partied, in general feeling sorry for myself. How could I do this? I didn't want to be with Andy. If I kept this baby I would do it on my own. I'd have to stay around here, which I hated, but I knew I could never move away with Andy staying here. He'd want as much involvement as I would, should I come to terms with having this baby.

Then one night, it happened.

I had a dream filled with baby's cries – my baby's cries. In my dream I went to pull my baby out of her crib. It was a girl. Her name was Adele. It was then, that I knew.

I could do this.

The Rose

Never say goodbye because saying goodbye means going away and going away means forgetting. ~ J. M. Barrie

My first pregnancy was a dark time in a lot of ways. I cried every day. I realize pregnancy makes one extra emotional anyway, but I had no idea what would happen once the baby was here. How would this work? I had made the decision to keep the baby, but now I was scared shitless about being a single mom. About being a mom, period. Adding to the emotional turmoil, my family had found out my grandpa was diagnosed with colon cancer. Since I had been teaching college classes only a few hours a day when I found out I was pregnant, I had the most flexible schedule in the family. My grandma had never gotten her driver's license, and with my grandpa's sickness, he wasn't allowed to drive. I was the designated driver at this time.

The cancer, or treatment, or something had changed my grandpa. He became very snappy and mean – just not himself. I drove to my grandparents' house to pick them up one day to take them on errands and my grandpa was especially difficult. He was yelling at my grandma in an incoherent way, and she would look at me and shake her head while trying to reason with him. Because I was so emotional and nauseated, I couldn't take much. I pulled back into their driveway, and my grandpa asked, "You're coming in?"

I felt completely spent. I said, "No, I can't." He stared at me a while, looking somewhat disappointed. I instantly felt guilty and thought that maybe I should go in for a while; I should take advantage of every second with him. But I couldn't. I told my dad later what happened, maybe to alleviate my guilt, I don't know. He seemed troubled by my description of grandpa that day and then talked to my grandpa and said grandpa wouldn't act like that again. I felt even worse after that. Now I had made two people I love feel bad.

Weeks later I held my grandpa's hand in the hospital and told him over and over I loved him. He was looking at me but couldn't speak due to the oxygen mask on his face. I was bawling, feeling helpless, overcome with sadness. That would be the last I saw him alive.

I'd moved into an apartment at that point, as my parents weren't crazy about the idea of living with them and raising a baby. I drove home from the hospital that day and parked the car in my apartment's car port. I cried, wailing, tears gushing down my face. For at least ten minutes. For a brief second, knowing everyone else was at work, I considered driving to Andy's house to fall into his arms and tell him I needed him, I needed someone. But I didn't. I went into my apartment and tried to deal with it on my own.

My grandpa died shortly after.

Though we had told him that I was pregnant before he died, I don't know if he comprehended it. He had always wanted to live to see me get married – he talked about it constantly. I felt guilty that he hadn't gotten to, that I had failed him in that way. Why couldn't I commit? I felt I was letting everyone down, not just him.

At the funeral visitation, I saw that a single white rose had been placed in the casket along with my grandpa. My mom told me my dad had the rose placed there as a gift from my unborn baby. I couldn't belief my dad had done that. That gesture made me cry more than anything. One, knowing that my grandpa would never meet her. Two, my dad hadn't seemed happy with my pregnancy at all up to this point. The rose was almost like his way of giving his blessing to me, too. My tears were a mixture of sadness and happiness.

It wasn't until months later, after I'd had our baby that Andy and I were sitting at my apartment drinking wine when I opened up and told him how guilty I felt for not going in my grandparents' house that day. I started crying thinking about it. This time Andy was there to hold me, his arms were there for me to fall into. But I still had the guilt. He told me to let it go, that I had been pregnant and not feeling well and I was being too hard on myself. Maybe he was right. Maybe everything happens for a reason.

Maybe my grandpa's looking down on us, smiling at the beautiful little girl who blossomed from that single white rose.

What to Expect When You Are Unexpectedly Expecting

Life is what happens to you while you're busy making other plans. ~ *John Lennon*

The fact that Andy and I weren't together during my pregnancy was not as simple as "I didn't want to commit." When I'd first met, Andy, I knew he was different. For one thing, he wasn't my "type" in a lot of ways. I was used to dating guys who often took longer than I did to get ready, who wore tight shirts and more than enough cologne. Andy had on a Guinness t-shirt when we met, and he sported a military buzz cut. My friend Jenny had introduced us and she'd pulled me aside right after the introductions, asking excitedly, "So what do you think? Isn't he cute?"

"Yeah!" I said. "He's just...not my type." And he wasn't. At least, not in every way. It was eventually revealed, however, that he did have a penchant for drinking. Like every other man I'd been with. If nothing else, it's always been the glue that's held my relationships together. As dysfunctional as that sounds.

Early on in our dating, I was supposed to meet Andy out one night with a few of our friends. He never showed up. One of his friends went to his house to check on him, and he was passed out drunk, having downed a bottle of Jack Daniel's. Red flag. Jenny dismissed it, saying, "Oh, so he got too drunk. He was probably just nervous to meet you and drank too much." Okay.

It soon became apparent, however, that Andy had some anger issues. Once we became exclusive, he got very possessive and territorial when it came to me. Another guy could breathe in my direction and Andy wanted to kick his ass. He always severely apologized the next day, and he really was the sweetest, most sensitive, romantic, caring man when he was sober. He showered me with cards, poems he wrote, teddy bears, and flowers on a daily basis. To someone with commitment issues, that can also help to successfully push a person straight out the door. So everything eventually became too much for me to handle, which contributed to the break-up.

I took walks every day when I was pregnant with Adele. I put my headphones on and walked, and walked, and walked. It was emotionally purging for me. I listened to the same songs over and over during that time period, and hearing one note of one of those songs takes me right back to that time. My pregnancy wasn't entirely horrible. In a lot of ways, it was the most serene I'd ever been. Knowing there was this tiny growing person inside me somehow calmed me down. I loved to lie on the couch in my apartment and rub my belly and feel the fluttering and kicking from within.

Even though we weren't together, Andy came to every single doctor's appointment. He either met me there or picked me up, and he brought doughnuts or hot chocolate for me most of the time. While these were nice gestures, I still didn't want to be with him.

I'd been hearing through some mutual friends that he'd been saying things like if he ever discovered I was dating anyone, he'd blow his head off. Nice. That wasn't helping his case if he wanted to be with me, and I certainly didn't need a psycho possessive case around my baby. I was now starting to think of myself as more of a protector of the little unknown person inside me than anything else.

Then, things changed. Andy picked me up one night close to my due date to go out to eat and talk about baby preparations. On the way home, I looked out the window at the snowflakes falling endlessly against the sky's black backdrop. Suddenly the reality of the situation hit me. I started crying and couldn't stop. He was rubbing my shoulder, asking what was wrong. I told him everything, how scared I was, how I resented him because I thought he'd tried to make this happen because he didn't want me to move. He immediately removed his hand when I talked about the resenting and getting me pregnant on purpose. I knew the baby would be here soon and I didn't want to bring her into the world with this mess of an undefined relationship happening. He seemed genuinely hurt that I'd suggest he would do something like this to someone intentionally, just because he wanted me around. I believed him (and knew all along it takes two, but when you're a crazy emotional pregnant mess, forget about logic). After that night, we started communicating more. It was strictly platonic, at least on my part.

The cold, snowy day that I went into labor he rode to the hospital with my mom and me, and he was there during the whole delivery. I wanted to punch the nurse I had, who quadrupled my pain when she tried to stick a needle in my hand. It took her ten minutes and felt like she was physically ripping the skin off while setting it on fire. Meanwhile, my mom was watching the monitor, marveling, "That was a big one!" with every intense contraction I had.

The epidural didn't work.

Andy was right there, clutching my hands, allowing me to dig my nails deep into his skin, my legs involuntarily scissor kicking back and forth, back and forth, back and forth. The pain was becoming unbearable. I was for sure I was going to die. This was how I'd die. It was also then that I started feeling a strong closeness to Andy. Not quite love, but...*something*. At the urging of Andy and everyone else in the room, I produced the final big push to get that baby out of me, and I'll never, ever, forget that moment of my baby being whisked away to a little table next to me. "She has hair!" they all exclaimed. I felt my eyes welling with tears of a happiness that I'd never felt before, one that I couldn't contain, one that was consuming every part of me, though I'd been in such excruciating pain merely seconds ago. This was so brand new. Everything about it. My baby did have hair. She had lots of black, curly hair. And I couldn't stop staring at her. Not for a second.

Adele was born at 9:54 p.m. on a Sunday. *Grey's Anatomy* was on. The next morning, Andy bought me flowers from our baby, Adele, and him. I was so touched by that. It was very sweet, and only added to my overflowing joy. He came into the hospital room, watching me hold her. He sat down beside me and brushed my hair behind my ear. I liked it. We both stared in awe at the beautiful, perfect little person we had created.

Once we took her home, he started spending the night at my apartment, sleeping on the couch and helping with Adele. We'd both wake up with her in the night and sit on opposite ends of the couch. One night he started rubbing my legs. It was nice. We weren't quite "together" yet, but we were in a warm, comfortable place.

A week after she was born, my mom and some of her friends came over. I was having my first glass of wine in nine months. I felt great. It was snowing, and I had a beautiful new baby who I was in love with. Andy was working at the fire department and sent me a text that said, "*I miss you both.*" I'll never forget that…because I missed him, too. I think that text was the beginning of my falling in love with him.

I miss you both.

He started buying six-packs of beer which we'd share at night…for me, after not drinking for nine months, it didn't take much at all to feel good. I think my feelings for him were growing stronger, and a little alcohol allowed me to loosen up and let it show.

One night we were looking at some of the children's books I'd stocked up on during my pregnancy, and I was showing him one of my favorites, *The Velveteen Rabbit*. We were sitting on the couch, and I was reading my favorite part, where the rabbit asks the skin horse how it feels to be real. Andy was holding a now sleeping Adele. It caught me off guard when he softly kissed me on the forehead. I stopped reading. It caught me off guard a little more when I realized I wanted him to *kiss me*, kiss me. He did. We started kissing more intensely. I was straddling him at that point, feeling more passion for a human being than I had ever felt in my life, not just on a sexual level, but on every level, when he asked, "Can I put her down?" I laughed and said yes.

So he carefully placed her in the bassinet.

I Walked the Line

Quick decisions are unsafe decisions. ~ Sophocles

I got a DUI in the fall of 2006. It was a very fun night. Well, up until the flashing lights behind me.

I went out with my friends Stephanie and Renee. We started out at a bar in the town next to mine, which is where we went out a lot. Some of the places we went were within walking distance from Renee's house, the place I usually stayed on those drunken nights.

As was typical, I hadn't eaten a lot before going out, because I didn't want to feel completely bloated as soon as I started drinking. So after two vodka and Red Bulls, I was already feeling half drunk. I felt like I was still okay to drive, though, so we left the first bar and went to the second establishment of the night.

That place was interesting. It was filled with "shady"-looking people. It was like every crazy misfit in town had crawled out from wherever they normally hid.

As soon as we walked in, every head turned to stare at us. It is typical for people in the area where I'm from to go out at night wearing baggy Tweety Bird sweatshirts or whatever someone might wear around the house to paint the living room. My friends and I, however, liked to dress up as if we were clubbing in NYC.

There was a DJ at this hole-in-the-wall dive bar for some reason, and after my friends and I started ordering drinks, we requested every fun dance song we could think of. "Pussy Control" is my favorite, so of course, that's what I requested first. The DJ, a *Jersey Shore*-looking reject, kept telling me how hot I was and asking if I'd sit on his lap. I repeatedly politely declined, so then he kept asking if he could have his picture taken with me. He would not let it go. So I let someone take our picture. This was the beginning of the weird madness that night.

In between dancing to our requested songs on our makeshift dance floor (and fighting off icky guys who tried to dry hump us) we sat at the bar drinking and smoking. It wasn't long before a group of somewhat scary-looking bikers started hitting on us. We always felt like supermodels going out to these places. A sketchy-looking woman next to us asked, "Have you ever had a Pink Pussy?" before she promptly ordered us all a strong, albeit tasty pink drink. I had on a soft angora sweater and she began to "pet" me. Her friend walked up to join us. "Pretty girls," they purred. My friends and I couldn't stop laughing.

It was then that one of the long-haired bikers leaped up on the bar in front of us, ripped off his shirt to reveal two pierced nipples, and started gyrating in our faces. "Oh my God!" we were screaming, while the bartender simply shrugged and kept pouring drinks. Apparently this was normal behavior.

Another guy there kept asking all of us how old we were, among other prying questions. I told him we were triplets. I loved lying to strangers anytime we went out. I used fake names, lied about my profession, and said I was from towns I've never even been to. That always made the night more fun.

It was the strangest, most random, yet hilarious night. By the time Renee's boyfriend showed up we were ready to leave, having had our fill of crazy. Again, I "thought" I felt okay to drive so we decided to go to Taco Bell, an end-of-the-drunken-night staple.

Big mistake.

We were on our way to Renee's, Eminem cranked full-blast, causing the whole car to shake with our bouncing around, when I saw the flashing lights behind me. I knew I was screwed. There was no point in getting upset at that point, I figured.

Renee quickly handed me a teensy stick of gum, which I shoved in my mouth, as if that was going to help. (Later on, I got to read the police report, and it had stated that I was "chewing on a large wad of gum." What the hell? It was one of those tiny pieces of Trident.) Stephanie acted like she was going to cry. "Shut up," I said, exasperatedly. "It doesn't matter now."

As soon as the highway patrol officer started talking, I asked, "Is this going to cost a lot? Because I have a lot of credit card debt." Everyone kind of sat in shock for a second, before bursting into laughter.

I really took the whole thing well. This might sound really weird, but I had fun with it. The second I got pulled over, I knew logically that I wasn't getting out of it, so this complete calm overtook my body. I was obviously still buzzed, too, so my mood was elevated. It probably hadn't registered yet. I had to do all of the field sobriety tests. I opted to remove my red stilettos to walk the line, which didn't prevent me from stumbling. (Damn you, vodkas and Red Bull. And Pink Pussy.)

The officer who pulled me over was actually very nice. I remained the sarcastic smartass I normally am. He took me and Stephanie to the station where I had to blow to reveal my blood alcohol content (Renee and her boyfriend had been dropped off) and then I had to do all this paperwork. Though Stephanie was at the station with me, we were sitting across the room from each other. She kept cupping her hands, presumably so Officer Alvarez couldn't see, and whispering things to me from the other side of the room. "Ummmm…you guys can just talk to each other," the officer said, amused, as we started laughing.

Officer Alvarez then went through the required paperwork with me, asking me questions like, "Do you have a glass eye?"

"Yes," I responded.

"Really?" he asked, incredulously.

"No." I stared at him.

"I'll take you next door!" he said, jokingly. (Next door was the holding cell, I presume.)

He was trying to write down what I was wearing, and he looked at my footwear. "What are those, high heels?"

"Ummmm...stilettos!" I responded, in a mock-annoyed tone. By this time we'd established a nice rapport and I knew I could say whatever I wanted to him.

On the ride home to Renee's house, we talked as if we were new college roommates getting to know one another. He learned I had a baby girl, and seemed surprised by this information. "You have a baby?" he asked, almost as if it mattered. Would he have given me a warning if he'd have known that to begin with?

Once I finally got home, I couldn't sleep, and my parents were up. I'd called my dad from the station, begging him not to get mad, but asking his advice on whether I should blow or not. My parents didn't seem mad. They knew I knew I'd made a mistake. Andy was at work when it happened, and my mom had to be the one to fill him in.

I had still been fine with the whole thing, in a good mood, even, until Andy came home and it really hit me. I collapsed into his arms and started crying. I suddenly felt like the biggest failure - as a wife, as a mother. The gravity of the whole situation hadn't sunk in the night before. Now I was realizing I wouldn't be able to drive anywhere for a long time, this would be on my record, this would cost a lot of money. I felt like a lowlife. Like a criminal.

Andy reassured me that I was not a bad person, that this was a lesson.

I ended up getting sentenced to having those DUI yellow plates on my car once I got work driving privileges. I felt like the biggest piece of shit on the planet at that point, with those scarlet letter plates on my car.

A few months after I got the DUI, I was at Meijer with my mom. She'd gone to the car, and I was in line checking out when I saw Officer Alvarez in line in front of me. "Hey!" I said, cheerfully. His pregnant wife next to him looked at me, at him, and back at me questioningly. "You gave me that DUI a while back!" I said, responding to the puzzled look on his face.

"Oh...hi!" He said. "Uh...how's it going?"

"Great!" I answered. "My mom's driving me around, so...it's good!"

I don't think he was used to the people he arrested being friendly toward him or greeting him too often in public, but I realize, he was only doing his job.

Did it suck? Yeah, it sucked. The whole six months I only had work-driving privileges really sucked. But it was my fault. And I don't want to even think about all the times I'd driven drunk before I got caught, or all the terrible things that could have happened as a result of my drunken driving. I was lucky. And I learned my lesson.

I told myself I wouldn't drink and drive ever again.

Emotional Nuptials

Any emotion, if it is sincere, is involuntary. ~ *Mark Twain*

A few months after a baby was born to the girl who had never wanted children, a funny thing happened.

The girl wanted to get engaged.

I didn't think I would ever feel the urge to make a lifelong commitment. The second ex-boyfriends had mentioned engagement rings, I was out the door. That shit was not for me. So it surprised everyone, especially me, when I found myself wanting Andy to propose.

I wasn't a total control freak about it, but I made sure to casually mention a time or two that if he were to pop the question, I wanted to be dressed up, and I didn't want it to happen in our town (meaning, "Don't ask me when I'm wearing sweats and we're watching *Seinfeld* re-runs on the couch).

Because of the "helpful suggestions" I'd provided, I totally knew I was getting engaged when Andy announced in June that we were taking a trip to Chicago and I should pack something dressy. Hello, little black engagement dress!

I was so excited. And nervous. We'd been to Chicago together before, and he'd said in the past that the first time we'd gone is when he started falling in love with me, so this was a special place for us. Even though I'd still been commitment-phobic at that point, it was the first time I'd taken a trip like that alone with a guy – ever. And we'd had a great time. So this trip was also an anniversary of sorts.

I was completely giddy about the whole trip. I knew what was coming. I went shopping beforehand for a new dress to wear when he proposed. I didn't end up finding one so I wore a black strapless I already had. I couldn't wait.

We got to Chicago, and like the last time we'd gone, we immediately hit the bars. The majority of our trips consisted of bar-hopping and not much else. Did you know Chicago also has museums? Someone told us that once. Anyway…

We went to the Hancock Building for our dressed-up night. It was unbelievable. I'm not sure what it was that I ate at the restaurant, but it resembled the food version of a Frank Lloyd Wright project. The view of the skyline alone was worth the money, though. Watching Andy nervously drink was adorable. Priceless.

After we ate, we went up to the lounge for an after-dinner drink. I, of course, had to order something we couldn't generally get where we were from, so I'm pretty sure my specialty martini ran him around the cost to fill up his gas tank. I kept waiting for it to happen. Every time he'd fidget I was sure it was the moment he was getting down on one knee.

All of a sudden he was insistent that we go to the observation deck. He really wanted to be there when the sun set, he said. Oh my God! This was it! I went to the bathroom and called my friend Renee from the stall, squealing, "I'm getting engaged!"

We rode the elevator up to the top and stepped out onto the breezy deck. The sun was starting to set.

It was perfect.

I walked up to the railing and leaned over, taking in the majestic skyline, the tiny windows twinkling in the skyscrapers like diamonds. I wanted to stay there forever.

"Sara," I heard Andy say, in a sing-songy, raised whisper. "Saaaaaaara." I knew what was about to happen, and I was suddenly freaking out – in a good way. I was so nervous and this moment was so huge. I couldn't look at him.

He said my name one more time and I turned to see the most sparkly, intensely beautiful piece of jewelry. And it was for me. An instant smile was glued to my face. I was in shock. Was this happening? Was that a ring?

He got down on one knee. "Will you marry me?"

"Yes!" I said, without having to think. He slipped the ring on my finger and I kissed him. I couldn't believe this!

We stayed up on the deck a while longer until the sun had completely set, and then we made our way down to solid ground, holding hands all the way. I called everyone; I had to share the news. "I'm engaged!" It was fabulous. I was high as a kite. A fleet of kites.

We went to a few bars that night, and I had to tell everyone there, too, so we scored tons of free drinks. It was great. By the end of the night I was pretty drunk, and continued to call people to spread the news. At least this was one night that the drunk dials were good news.

I was in shock for so long after that night. I loved having that ring on my finger. I stared at it on the steering wheel while I was driving. I stared at it while I worked out on the stair climber. I couldn't wait to be Andy's wife. I loved being his fiancée.

It wasn't too long of an engagement. We got married on St. Patrick's Day, 2007. St. Patrick's Day had been the first time we'd gone to Chicago together.

I went to get my nails done before our wedding rehearsal the night before. In the *middle* of doing my nails, my soft-spoken Asian nail tech mumbled something about how she'd be right back. I figured she went to get more cotton balls or something, so I nodded and continued to tap my feet and watch the clock, as I didn't have much time to get to the church. At least 20 minutes later, she walked in the front door with a little boy; like she just left in the middle of my appointment to get her kid from daycare. So I was late to my wedding rehearsal, which caused its own set of problems.

The rehearsal dinner was not good. In every way. I didn't want to be hungover for my wedding day, but I did have to have a buzz to get through it. Later that night, I was up waiting for Andy to call like he said he would, and he didn't. I didn't sleep at all. I knew he'd had a lot to drink, and since I'm someone who is fantastic at imagining every possible horrific scenario, I was crazy worried. The next day he said he'd left his phone in his truck. We got into a tiny fight about it.

Then I bawled on my wedding night, at the end of the night. In the hotel room. It was supposed to be just Andy and me, but I was feeling so emotional; I wanted Adele with us. I knew we were leaving for the honeymoon soon and I wanted to spend time with her. I still had on my wedding dress, and I was sobbing. I think it was a release, after everything leading up to the wedding. I was drunk and drained in every way possible. So much energy goes into this one day, and then it flies by, and like that – it's over.

I did eventually stop crying and insist Andy and I have sex since it was our wedding night. I'm romantic like that.

And Then There Were Four

Call it a clan, call it a network, call it a tribe, call it a family. Whatever you call it, whoever you are, you need one. ~ Jane Howard

The weekend before I found out I was pregnant with Eleanor, I had been drunk. A lot. Much like the weekend before I found out I was pregnant with Adele. It's not like I did it on purpose. My kids seem to have turned out okay.

The years leading up to this pregnancy were rocky. Andy and I had brought up divorce more than once. I had been going out a lot with my friends, which I think he resented, but his way of communicating at the time was to keep everything bottled up inside until he got drunk and exploded at me out of nowhere. At one point, I pretty much had one foot out the door, already starting to plan how I'd live on my own. I, of course, used alcohol as a means of escape, and coupling that with going out with my friends equaled trouble. Neither Andy nor I were doing anything constructive to help the relationship. There were a lot of screaming matches during this time, usually involving alcohol.

That all changed when we started seeing a counselor.

I was skeptical at the start of counseling. I felt like I had personally let Andy know for the trillionth time how much his behavior upset me, and he wasn't changing it, so I wasn't sure that he'd change it now. I knew I wasn't perfect, either, though, and I had to be willing to suspend disbelief in order for this to work.

Dr. M. is amazing. I really do feel that he saved our marriage. During the course of counseling, it became more than apparent that Andy had major anger issues, which really only manifested when he drank. So the first step to conquer this, we were told by Dr. M., was to have Andy keep an anger journal…and stop drinking for a while. I was so relieved. During the next few months Andy became a completely different person. He learned how to control his anger, what the source of it was, and at that point, he could incorporate alcohol again.

He didn't drink for about three months. I was very nervous when he started again, afraid this whole experiment wouldn't work. The night we were out before the pregnancy realization, we encountered a "test." Andy had always been super jealous and possessive; if he saw a guy even talk to me, he'd want to fight him. He'd started working on his anger, though. So we were at a bar when I went up to get a drink. Some wasted guy came up behind me, basically dry-humping me from behind. I helplessly glanced across the room at Andy, waiting for him to swoop in and save me like Superman. Andy saw me, but stood there watching. That's when I realized he was taking this counseling seriously. This guy wasn't leaving me alone and Andy wasn't helping me, so I turned around and shoved him as hard as I could. He fell backwards into his friends, their drinks flying everywhere.

When I got back to Andy and expressed my disbelief that he chose this time of all times to not intervene, and he said, "You can take care of yourself. I saw you." I knew he was a changed man.

So when I showed him the positive pregnancy test, it was a good thing. All the time I'd been spending getting drunk with my friends wasn't good for our relationship, and now he was working on improving himself. Both of my pregnancies couldn't have come at better times. They both saved me at different points in my life, in different ways.

It was great to be with Andy during this pregnancy. When I was pregnant with Adele, it was so hard being alone and not knowing the future. I wanted to have a pregnancy with Andy to have what we hadn't experienced before. He got to feel the baby kick this time, know how I was feeling, be fully present with it all.

I really tried to hold onto those nine months and appreciate them, knowing this would most likely be my last pregnancy. I remember thinking there was no way I could love anyone as much as I loved Adele; I couldn't imagine it. I tried to play with her as much as I could before Eleanor was born, cherishing the last moments that she'd be an only child.

I had Eleanor, and an amazing thing happened. All my fears about not being able to love another human being as much as I loved Adele disappeared, and my heart grew to accommodate her. While at the time I couldn't imagine having another child to take care of, ever since Eleanor's been here I can't imagine a life without her.

Both of my pregnancies forced me to change my lifestyle, if only temporarily. I think they happened for a reason, or various reasons. Maybe to show me what unconditional love is. Maybe to show me that I do have a maternal side.

Maybe to show me that I could live sober.

Gasoline Rainbows

If you're going through hell, keep going. ~ *Winston Churchill*

At least I still had a slight buzz going when I was fired and escorted off the grounds by security.

I didn't want to take the job at the college. I knew what it was like there. I didn't want to take it, but it was full-time with benefits, and I didn't exactly have people beating down my door offering me that every day. So I reluctantly went to the interview and feigned interest the best I could.

This school, as I would soon learn, was not at all like a real college. It pretended to be. It called itself a university, but what I encountered in the classroom – and from the administration – was nowhere near what a college should be. I'm pretty sure I have PTSD from the whole experience.

I was interviewed by two of the like 27 unqualified deans they have working there. All together I think they comprise maybe 60% of a complete working brain, so it works out pretty well for them, I guess.

The interview was a joke. I nodded and smiled a lot through gritted teeth, all the while wanting to cry at the fact that I would soon be working there (I knew I was the only one being interviewed, and they were desperate). At the interview I was told I'd be teaching English, psychology, and cultural diversity courses, among others. I had some ideas for the diversity class, and I asked if I'd be able to bring in guest speakers.

"Sure!" answered one of the deans. "You can bring in a Hispanic or black person, but this school's not ready for a gay person. Them's not a culture." He continued, "Them's not a culture anyway, but this school's not ready for that. There was a gay guy who came and talked one time, and you should've seen these guys. They wanted to beat him up. We can't have that here."

What. The. Fuck.

I didn't know whether to be more appalled at his inability to grasp the English language or his blatant homophobic remarks. And this was who I'd be working for?

The other dean had been looking over my resume and discovered we lived in the same area. He asked, "So you're not one of those women who are in front of me on the road, holding up traffic putting on your makeup, are you?"

"Um, no," I stammered, amazed that between the two of them, they'd managed to offend homosexuals and women in thirty seconds' time. "I put on my makeup at home."

I couldn't wait to work for these homophobic, misogynistic pea-brained assholes. And this was the beginning.

There were zero admission requirements to get into this school and it was widely known that admissions reps lied to prospective students (and I partied with a rep one night, who drunkenly told me this) to get them to attend, so we're talking the cream of the crop. They were going to school to learn various vocations, mostly dealing with cars, and I was responsible for teaching them the parts of speech. As you might imagine, this did not go well.

For the most part, my students could give two shits about English, which is fine; I had to take things like astronomy in college, which didn't relate to my literature degree. But I was not raised by wolves in a cave somewhere, as apparently the better part of this student body was, because common decency was not common. Whatsoever.

My students were primarily male. Once in a while I had a random girl, but she usually blended in pretty well with the guys. For the most part, these were rude, obnoxious, idiotic, uncultured, illiterate, redneck assholes. And that's me being nice about it.

My Last Rock Bottom

When I would walk into the building they'd stare as if they'd never seen a woman before, and they stared at me the whole time I walked down the hall. And it was a long hall. Sometimes I had to walk through shop areas, wearing safety goggles, and they'd whistle or yell things – but that was anywhere I was walking on campus. I'm pretty sure if it had a vagina, they were whistling at it.

Being in the classroom was a nightmare. I'd get asked things like, "Have you ever worked at Hooters?" I was once told by a student that another student wanted to "tea bag" me. (If you don't know what that is, Google it.) I had a student tell me one time, "My friend Mark is in your morning class and he said he can never pay attention to what you're saying because he's thinking about bending you over the desk the whole time." Another student reassured me, "Oh, ignore them. They just think of you as the teacher from Varsity Blues." My student evaluations would come back mostly full of crude comments about my looks, not my teaching ability. It was degrading. Embarrassing.

And as far as teaching ability goes, well, it was not easy. Aside from being sexually harassed on a daily basis, the students were primarily dumbasses. I don't mean because they didn't get A's in my class, either - which, by the way, is hard not to do; as long as you have a pulse you can pass my class - but they were rude and inconsiderate. I had to yell all the time for them to shut up so I could teach, and they never stopped complaining. Ever.

If they didn't smoke, they chewed, and they all kept spit bottles on their desks which they elegantly spat in all through class. Classes were two hours long. I generally tried to start late, take an extra long break in the middle, and end early. I called in sick whenever I could.

It was during my stint at this school that I started drinking extra heavily. Every night after class, (oh, and I taught until 11 pm, by the way) I'd race home to my wine. Usually I'd text Andy first, telling him to have it poured and ready for me when I got home.

It was also during this time that I started getting severely depressed, not wanting to get out of bed - sometimes because I was hungover, but mostly because I hated my job so much. I had perpetual knots in my stomach. I dreaded going there, I dreaded getting out of my car and feeling them all watch me walk everywhere I went. I was seeing Dr. M. on my own then, and he suggested I tell my family doctor about my depression. So I was prescribed anti-depressants. But I didn't stop the drinking, so the depression didn't budge. I was one giant, depressed, drunken mess.

I was crying to and from work before it was all said and done. Sometimes I drank on my lunch break. I hated it so much, but I didn't have a way out. We needed the money. I would beg Andy, crying and pleading to him to let me quit.

We needed the money.

One thing (the only thing) that made the job bearable was when I'd take my class to the computer lab (composition courses weren't normally taught in computer labs because that would've made too much sense) and I'd talk to the computer lab technicians, who were a handful of "computer geeks" – very intelligent, hilarious guys. I loved talking to them. I looked forward to computer lab night like I looked forward to Christmas. I ended up becoming very good friends with them.

Meanwhile, the job was going more and more downhill. The rest of my life was a complete mess. The job was affecting everything. Andy and I were having problems because I was miserable and remedying it by getting plowed as often as humanly possible, making some unwise decisions about who I hung out with in the process. Some of my good friends seemed to be fading out of the picture because, as one of them put it, "It's just not enjoyable to talk to you. You're always so negative." And I was. I didn't like anything in my life at that point.

I became completely fatalistic about my job; I didn't care if I lost it because I hated it, and Andy wasn't going to let me quit. I knew I was being watched at the school; there were a couple of deplorable, two-faced women working there (let's call them "Bitchface" and "Cuntface") who had it in for me from day one and told on me for everything, trying to get me into trouble for anything I did. It didn't matter what it was. The week I got fired I got in trouble for like ten things, which I'm assuming was part of their way of building a case against me to justify the firing. I don't even remember now what those little things were, but I know they were things every faculty member there did and didn't get in trouble for.

Part of my problem is and always has been being too trusting of people. I need to be more private and guarded, but that's not me. One might think that with everything that's happened to me, I'd change how I am. Even though I've experienced the unfortunate betrayal of countless duplicitous people, I like the fact that I'm open and trusting. Yes, it's caused problems. It's also allowed me to make some great friends.

So here's the thing. I was friends on Facebook with way too many co-workers. It hadn't crossed my mind that one of my "friends" would have such a sad, pathetic little life that she'd print off pages and pages of my Facebook wall, staple them into a tidy little book with a cover page, and anonymously turn it in to the 27 deans.

I post whatever is on my mind, which is my style, and at the time, hating every single aspect of that piece of shit school was what was on my mind. Here is an example of something that got me in trouble: "Once again, boys, revving your engines for five minutes and taking off like a bat out of Hell does not give you a bigger penis." That's what every single one of these knuckleheads did every night in the parking lot. Never did I mention the school, and there was nothing in the handbook justifying my being fired and not given a warning. I wanted out of there, so I didn't fight it, but I think I could have. And won. The reason they actually cited for firing me was "sexual comments to students on Facebook." Because I was friends with the computer lab workers. And one time we were coming up with fake porno titles. (One of the lab guys also hated his job, so he suggested Andy and I make porn and he could direct it. Naturally.)

A contributing factor in my mind is, right before I got fired I didn't get my paycheck when I was supposed to. I told the deans, who did nothing. I told the university president, who did nothing. My bank account was overdrawn because of it. I complained about it because it was wrong.

I knew I was being fired before it happened. I was teaching my night class when I got an e-mail from the HR woman, asking if I could meet with her early the next morning. Right then I felt my face grow hot and my heart beat out of my chest. I knew I was being fired. And right after that night class, I went to my "office," where another instructor said, "Sara, I hear you're leaving us! Bitchface is teaching your courses for the rest of the quarter?" I felt my face grow even hotter.

"What?" I asked, incredulous.

"Oh," she said, realizing I hadn't known about this. "Uh, never mind." I kept pressing her, and she kept saying, "I'm sure it's a mistake, I'm sure it's not true." So the deans had already lined up Bitchface to cover my classes! It was official.

I was a wreck that night up until the next morning. I knew I was being fired, so I got up and made mimosas. When I got to the "meeting" with the HR woman, both deans who had hired me were there. They handed me the booklet of my own Facebook updates, highlighted, circled, underlined. All I could say was, "I figured this was it." They seemed shocked. I was so calm about it. Because I knew. What really pisses me off is the fact that I cried before the meeting was all said and done. I hadn't wanted them to see me weak. And I'm still not completely sure why I cried. Maybe because I was so drained from this job. And it was over.

I have to say it was a new experience to be escorted out by security like I'm some kind of criminal. My e-mail was immediately disabled; never mind that I had important information on there that I needed to retrieve.

Because every one of my co-worker friends who had ever commented on anything I wrote on Facebook either got fired or in trouble, they stopped talking to me. Like it was my fault who commented. I learned quickly who my real friends were from that job. And they were pretty much no one.

So what did I learn from this? I'm not sure, except that life's too short to be miserable. I am very suspicious of co-workers now. Especially women. I know alcohol played an integral part in my getting fired, although I didn't belong there anyway. Even when I was sober (because of pregnancy) I hated it. I'm pretty sure the only reason I had Eleanor was to get maternity leave. (Of course, she was cute, so we kept her.)

I had to try and focus on anything remotely positive when I worked there, just so I could keep going. When I'd walk across campus, I would always look down and stare at the gasoline rainbows all the cars had left behind. I appreciated the beauty of each little pool of iridescent colors, and for a second, I forgot where I was.

I was content.

The Panic Attack

Fear makes us feel our humanity. ~ Benjamin Disraeli

It was September 12, 2011. I had a new job at a different college, but had called in to work the day before because of a massive sinus infection. We had shown our house the day before (it'd been for sale for a few months by then, and although I didn't want to leave the house, I wanted to leave the town) so we had to clean everything top to bottom, and I felt like complete shit. So I had known the night of September 11 that I had the next day off.

I was lying in bed with Andy that night, glad that I could sleep in and hopefully not feel like death much longer, but also somewhat panicked at the idea of having to go back to class ever.

I'd been teaching a business communications class for the past two months, something I knew nothing about – I had never taken a business course – yet I was expected to dispense such pertinent information like how a resume should look (mine hadn't been updated in the ten years since I'd made it), how one should conduct oneself at an interview (coming from a walking "don't" – really – everything in the textbook that said "Don't" I had done at every interview), and basically I had no clue what I was doing. Classes were four hours long.

I have an MA in literature, and I've enjoyed teaching literature– somewhat – but overall feel I was not meant to instruct. I'm way too uptight. I think too much about what people think. *Do the students like me? Do my co-workers like me? Does my department chair like me? Am I doing something wrong? I am; I know it. I'm in trouble. I suck; I suck at life; everybody hates me.*

This is a typical dialogue in my head. It's lovely to be me. Shortly after the incident I'm about to describe, I was diagnosed with generalized anxiety disorder, which solves many of life's mysteries for me. (Like in third grade, my deathly fear of the nasty, gag-inducing, shock-to-the system fluoride treatments we were expected to endure. I would worry and worry the night before. I'd cry. I would, like, hyperventilate. I'm actually starting to now, thinking about it. Anyway.)

So teaching basically isn't good for my psyche. I care too much. I know, logically, that I can never make everyone happy, or please everyone all of the time. I know that. Yet professions like this, where so many people are relying on me and I feel I have all these people to please – professions like these are an anxiety attack waiting to happen for me.

I had been teaching around eight years leading up to this pinnacle event, which sounds like a long time – and really, it is. I don't know how I did it, honestly. Well, I guess I do know. I was hungover at least 25% of the time, drunk maybe 5-10% of the time, on Ativan or Xanax 5% of the time, and otherwise I think I really did try to do a good job. I'm only kidding! I was probably drunk more like 20% of the time.

The hungover/drunk parts were early in my career – I was still a huge partier, as were my friends, except I had to get up early the next day and teach. Hence, sometimes, I'm pretty sure, counts as the "still drunk" part. I showed a lot of movies.

Teaching is what I'd been doing since college graduation (in addition to bartending – both will engineer one for alcoholism, by the way) even though I never once felt that I wanted to be a teacher. Of anything. But what else do you know with an MA in literature when you live in the middle of a cornfield? So there I was, an adjunct instructor anywhere and everywhere at the time. Getting fired at my last teaching job had amped up my already high anxiety, so at my current job, with every little thing that happened, I was convinced I was getting the axe. Not good.

Teaching was already giving me high anxiety because of my sick, twisted thinking in which I want everyone to like me, and then when an overbearing administration is thrown in, with at times, completely unmanageable students (yes, at the college level – we're not talking Stanford here). Throw on top of that a class I'm not qualified for and know nothing about, and...

I lost my shit.

I woke up on September 12, feeling an odd, intense mixture of relaxation and panic. Feeling something I'd never felt before. The night before, when I'd been in bed with Andy, he wanted to watch the 9/11 footage, much to my displeasure. I think it's good to remember...but I think our culture borderlines on obsession with the remembrance. I had avoided watching any footage of it at all, all weekend, because I didn't want to "relive" those memories. But he turned it on and we were watching it. I had a half glass of apple wine, thinking the fruit would help my sinus infection – okay, really, I had to be a little buzzed to watch this footage. If I'm being completely honest, I had to be buzzed every night at that point. I also had a cornucopia of pills to help me sleep, help my anxiety, help my sinus infection.

Tons and tons and tons of pills.

I snuggled up to him in bed, horror-stricken, and watched the special on the Discovery Channel that was filmed from the firefighters' point of view, naturally. I, like everyone else alive, had watched the footage the day it had happened ten years ago, along with every other year when they showed anniversary footage. It's not that I didn't know it was real any of those times. But this time, lying next to my firefighter, it suddenly became *too* real.

I watched these first responders on TV rush into the skyscrapers with black smoke billowing out, and for the first time, I really let myself feel what I'd known all these years Andy does for a living. Since, again, we live in the middle of a cornfield, he goes to fires, but nothing too big, hardly ever, and none I'd ever really had to worry about.

I mean, I do worry, but I never really, really let myself panic. Watching the 9/11 footage that night in bed with him really hit me on a visceral level, more than it had watching it any other time. I stared, mesmerized, at the TV, watching these brave men go inside, knowing there was a good chance they'd never return, knowing that - I couldn't believe that could be my husband. That could be him.

And then came the oh-so-familiar inner monologue downward spiral.

I wasn't nice enough to him. Would he know how much I loved him? What if he never knew how much I really loved, respected, and admired him?

What if he didn't know I couldn't imagine a life without him?

What if he never knew, because I was always sarcastic? I never just took his head in my hands and told him how amazing he was and how lucky I felt to have him, how blessed I was that he picked me. What if he never knew that, and then one day he died rescuing some stranger, saving someone's life? And what had I done with my life? What had I done to live heroically?

I was a drunk addicted to pills. He deserved better. Way better.

As we continued to watch the footage, I scooted closer to him and started really squeezing him, holding him as close as possible. The towers were really blazing now; you could see tiny images of people falling or jumping from windows.

"What do you think happens when you die?" I asked Andy.

"I don't know," he said.

"I mean...what happens? Your body's still there, but...where do you...go?"

"I don't know, Sara," he said, somewhat exasperatedly, as he often did when I took us down my lines of thinking.

"I mean...look at those people falling...do they feel it? Do they feel it when they die?"

"They die as soon as they hit the pavement."

"So it doesn't feel like anything? I mean, what about falling?"

"Well, they feel the falling."

"What's that like? Like when we rode the roller coaster at Kings Island? Like that?"

"It's a little bit faster than that, Sara," he said, rubbing his temples.

"So then...I mean...when you die...when they die, when they actually hit the concrete, it's just...nothing? I mean, what's that feel like? Just, you're here, you're alive, and then nothing? What's nothing feel like?"

"I don't know, Sara," Andy said, and I knew I'd been nearing his breaking point with this. "How am I supposed to know this? No one knows this. No one knows this except people who've died, and they can't tell us."

"Well," I started, "people have written books about it..."

"Yeah...people have said they died and saw the light..."

"But how do we know if they're lying?" I asked.

"I don't know, Sara." This is the line he probably says the most in our relationship.

"I just...I just can't...I can't wrap my head around it. Like what it feels like. Were those people scared?"

"I'm sure they were, Sara."

"But like, what about my cousin, Andy...I mean...what happens...where did he go?"

"Again, Sara, people have different beliefs, but none of us knows until we die ourselves."

My cousin, who was only 34 years old, (who is also named Andy) had recently died of what was discovered after the fact of pulmonary embolism. I'd been thinking of it nonstop ever since. It was surreal. I had talked to him on Facebook the night before. I couldn't believe it. It wasn't real. So I'd been thinking a lot about death lately, and wondering what happens when you die.

I didn't sleep at all really that night...and the sleep I did get was broken, and full of images of people falling from the Twin Towers.

The next morning, though I was exhausted, I was awake – awake with that eerie feeling of calm/fear. Andy was at work, Adele was at school, and Eleanor was asleep. I tried to go back to sleep, but my brain would simply not shut off. Images of the 9/11 footage still haunted me. So naturally I did what any normal, sane, sleep-deprived, anxiety-ridden person at eight in the morning would do: I YouTubed 9/11 footage. I found one video titled "People falling from tower" and I clicked on it. I was obsessed. I had to understand, with dread and knots in my stomach, I had to better comprehend what happened. What this all meant.

The video had no sound. It was perhaps the most disturbing thing I've ever seen, ever. Chilling. The footage was actually pretty close up. You could see people clinging for dear life, literally, to the sides of windows, before eventually giving up and letting go, as flames and ebony smoke wafted out around them. One by one, they let go, and flailed wildly in the sky, all the way down. I couldn't stop watching. I was transfixed.

At first, like the day 9/11 actually happened, I was in denial, or simply desensitized by all the violence TV and movies bombard us with, and I wasn't deeply affected. All of a sudden, however, sitting propped up, cross-legged on my bed at eight in the morning, amber sunlight streaming through my window, hair uncombed, bags under my eyes; all of a sudden I started to get it. Something struck a major nerve. I watched these people fall, silently, mouths agape, screaming for help, for mercy, for God, for salvation, and I looked around my bedroom. I was depressed, the same way I woke every day, but I was also something else. I suddenly wondered, as I often did, but really truly wondered what the point of life was. I didn't like my job, I felt I was a lousy wife, I thought my kids deserved a mommy who always wanted to play, who wasn't irritable. They deserved someone who cared about every little thing they did, not one who pushed them off to the side periodically because her despair was too all-consuming.

What was the point of it all?

And, if as Andy said, one didn't feel the impact of hitting the pavement, it seemed like the best solution. Living nowhere near skyscrapers I figured pills would be the way to go for me. I had taken so many the night before, not to die, but perhaps enough that a few more would've done it. I didn't want to commit suicide. I didn't want to do that to my family. If it were an accident though, then…

I looked back at the computer screen, at the silent wail of victims and again began questioning the purpose of this all. My cousin was a great man, a man who, regrettably, I really, really wished now I'd have reached out to and gotten to know better. I felt terrible about that. So why did he have to die, and all these other people – people like me – people who I felt were doing no one any good – why was I allowed to live?

My cousin had been a teacher, and a great one. He had helped me one time with a psychology course I was teaching, and I could tell how much he really passionately cared about teaching. He gave me stacks of books, handouts, told me about several experiments I could implement in class. I'd never seen him light up or talk more than he did that day.

I wanted to stand up at his funeral and talk about that day he had helped me with teaching. We had the opportunity at the funeral to say how my cousin Andy had affected us. I wanted to, but I was already crying and knew I'd bawl and it would have taken five years to get it out of me. Still. Now I wished I'd said it.

Why was he gone and I was here? I was a terrible teacher, I felt. Because of my depression, I felt that my heart wasn't in it. Teachers should be like him, not me. And if this is my life, unfulfilled in my job, thinking my husband deserves better, thinking my children deserve better; if this is it, if this is as good as it gets, as Jack Nicholson's character, Melvin Udall wonders in one of my favorite movie scenes ever, then, why?

Why continue living in the daily hell I was in, the daily prison of existing in my own body, my own brain? What was the point of enduring this pain every day when, as it happened on 9/11, your life could end without warning some Tuesday morning after you'd arrived at work?

I didn't want to be here.

I stared at the computer screen again, watching the people topple down, one by one, to their deaths.

Suddenly I couldn't breathe.

All of a sudden I felt very weird. Like super hyper/couldn't stand being in my own skin/hard to breathe/couldn't stop moving weird. I was jumpy. Jittery. Shaking. I hadn't slept at all, yet my brain was far too wired to sleep. I felt as if I were to lie down and try to sleep I might die. It sounds strange, I'm sure. What really kicked the "weirdness" into overdrive were the last few people I watched fall from the towers sort of set my breathing into heaving, with chest pains. From there I felt as if the whole world was closing in on me. I'd be fine for a second, and then all of a sudden this weird, alternate reality thing would happen where nothing seemed real. I was me. I was fine. And then I wasn't me. I didn't know who I was. My world was closing in on me again.

I thought I was dying.

I called my mom. "I feel…weird." I said, quite eloquently, considering the circumstances.

"Okay…what do you mean, weird?" A perfectly reasonable response.

"I mean, like…I don't know how to explain it. Like…weird, like I'm not okay. Like something's wrong."

"Well…"

"Like, I took a bunch of cold medicine last night and this morn-"

"Well some of that medicine always does that to me, too. Allergy medicine and cold medicine make me feel light-headed. Maybe if you try to go back to slee-"

"I can't"

"Okay…"

"I mean, I know I can't. It could be medicine, but it's weirder than that...it's like...something's not right. Like I feel like I'm dying or I might pass out or something..."

This went on a few more minutes before my mom urged me to call Janis, a friend in town who could come stay with me until my mom got there. She also urged me to call my aunt Darlene, who is a nurse.

As soon as Janis got there, she came upstairs to where I was on the bed, my knees pinned against my chest, rocking back and forth, wearing my t-shirt and Andy's boxers.

"Hi," she warmly greeted me. "How are you feeling?" Her expression changed from pleasant to concerned.

"I'm...not good," I said.

She sat up on the bed with me, watching me rock myself back and forth. I couldn't stop moving or shaking.

"Do you want a massage? Would that make you feel better?"

"Sure," I answered, a sign of how bad off I really was. I mean, I love massages but would normally be too self-conscious to let a friend lube me up.

She found some chamomile lotion by my bed while I lay face down. It was surreal. Surreal, as in, I knew this was happening, but I was still having this sort of out-of-body experience. I think her kneading of my muscles did help, but my brain was still in overdrive.

"If your mom walks in we'll just tell her we were playing doctor," Janis joked, and I mustered a laugh. The massage felt great, but I still didn't.

I called my aunt once my mom got there and Darlene felt that I should go to the ER. It was her son, Andy, my cousin, who had just died, and I think more than anything at this point, the whole "better safe than sorry" mantra was ringing loud and clear for all of us. Darlene herself had just been diagnosed with breast cancer and had undergone a double mastectomy. (Personally, I still don't know how she gets out of bed in the morning. She's phenomenal.) I described my symptoms to her on the phone as I'd told my mom, "It's like, all of a sudden, nothing's real. I know this sounds fucked up – well, sorry for using the 'fuck' word, but – but I feel like maybe I should go in the psych ward?"

"No," Darlene said. "I don't think you need to go to the psych ward. I think you're having a panic attack. Your Grandpa Sproul used to get them and so did your cousin Russell."

Good to know.

So Darlene said she would meet us at the ER. On the way, I called Dr. M., to whom I also described the symptoms. He said, "You're having your first real-blown panic attack, girl!" It was bizarre. I asked him if it was at all like being high, and he said it kind of was. I also told him I kind of thought maybe I should be in the psych ward, and he said, "No, you're having a panic attack." I can vividly recall the conversation I had with him, and yet it's as if it was someone else, and not me.

The whole entire experience was so bizarre. I know I was wearing the same clothes I'd worn to the hospital to have my babies…the kind of clothes you wear when comfort is your only concern. The difference was, when I was leaving the house to give birth, I did my hair and makeup. I glanced at myself in the mirror before heading to the ER for the panic attack, shuddered at what I saw – unkempt, greasy hair, broken out face, sunken eyes, yet had less than zero motivation to do anything about any of it. Plus, I was shaking too badly to do anything about it if I had given a shit that I might run into a former student or past one-night stand. I physically could not do anything about it.

In my mom's van, on the way to the ER, I tried to calm my hands and keep them from involuntarily shaking, but it wasn't working. When we got there and I got out, I screamed, "Stop the van!"

"It's stopped, Sara," my mom said calmly.

So now I was hallucinating. Perfect.

As soon as my aunt saw me, who has always remarked how good I look, although that's at Christmases, family weddings, and events where makeup, non-stained attire, and bathing are an integral part, she said, "You don't look good."

"I don't feel good," I said. She gave me a hug and we sat down to work on paperwork. My mom was parking the car with Eleanor. Darlene had to fill out my forms since my fingers were still involuntarily shaking beyond writing capacity.

Once I got called back I lay down a long time and talked to a lot of different doctors, nurses, nursing students, interns, and I don't know who else. At the end of the day they sent me home with Flonase and Xanax, because I had called in to work that day for a legit sinus infection, which had still been there. Who goes to bed with a sinus infection and wakes up with a panic attack?

I do.

I do remember, before I was released, the counselor who came in and spoke to me...she looked like Claire Danes, for one thing, which I would have told her, but didn't really want to bother with it, as I was still having those intermittent waves of panic where I thought I was going to die and all. But she also seemed to really listen. Not that any good came of it. I mean, besides, "Here's your Xanax; have a nice day."

Before the counselor came, I talked to my aunt in the ER room.

"This is so weird," I said.

"Yeah, it is a little weird," she nodded wistfully, with her arms clasped around her legs, which were crossed, the foot on top dangling. "But it's good that you're getting everything checked out. So you just took a lot of cold medicine?"

"Yeah. I mean, and sleeping pills. Both. Probably too much of both. I just wanted to feel better and wanted to sleep and nothing was working."

"Well, I think," she said, "that you took too much cold medicine maybe."

"Yeah. Oh, and wine. I drank some wine. Not much...but..." I said, and then there was silence. We both became lost in our own dark thoughts, I think, trying to grasp the reality of the situations. Trying to understand life.

"I think I might go check out Compassionate Friends, a support group for parents who have lost children," Darlene said, half-smiling through tears that seemed to be on the brink of falling.

"I think that's a great idea," I said. "I was thinking about that the other day. Of something like that."

I was sitting up now, in the hospital bed, with my knees pulled to my chest, my hospital gown pulled tightly beneath my toes. I was holding my legs and rocking back and forth.

"I just…I guess I feel like I try to be happy…I try to be what everyone wants me to be but…I'm not." I started crying, letting the tears fall down my cheeks in rivulets until they splashed onto my papery hospital gown. "And then, I always wonder, I mean…what is the point?" I wiped my nose and eyes and looked over at Darlene.

"I know," she said. "It's like waking up every day in Bizarro World."

"Yeah," I said. "I don't understand, like…what is the purpose? Why am I here? Why do things happen? I wished I would have talked to Andy more. I think we had a lot in common."

"I think you did. I wish I knew why things happen, too."

"Yeah…"

"Sara?"

"Yeah?"

"You make sure you tell the counselor the stuff you told me…about how you feel and wondering what the point of it all is."

"Oh, I will," I said. "I don't hold back."

"That's good. Well I should probably head back to work. I love you," Darlene said as she stood up to hug me.

"I love you too," I said, holding back more tears.

And then I watched one of the most remarkable women I have ever known leave the room.

I was sent home and my parents stayed at my house a while to help with the kids. I gradually started to feel better, and once I got some decent, consistent sleep, the panic completely subsided. At least, for the time being.

My Last Rock Bottom

The wound is the place where the Light enters you. ~ Rumi

Being drunk is a lot like wearing armor, I imagine. I've never actually worn armor. But I know that being drunk does make me feel invincible, protected, like I can do anything and it'll be okay. I have an excuse for whatever I do. It wasn't always that way, but it got to the point where the beginning of a night involving drinking started out with me feeling like a bundle of nerves. I was nervous for myself. I didn't know how the night would progress or end up or what I'd do, if I'd do anything that would turn out to be unforgivable, if I'd make a complete ass out of myself, sob uncontrollably, become a hedonistic lunatic, generally act like someone who had no business being married.

This is why I felt safest drinking around people who drank as much, or more, than I did, and who acted as badly as I did when I drank. I think we really fueled each other. On our own, I don't think my friends were too crazy. But throw me in the mix, and suddenly everybody is insane.

I had gotten very comfortable with these people – I could say or do anything around them and it'd be okay. This might sound ideal, how friendships should be, except, throw large quantities of alcohol in the mix, and I know now that can sometimes get out of hand.

I think we had more or less simply become enablers of each other. I loved hanging out with them, as they were smart, funny, and nice. The insanity progressed, the more we hung out. It was practically guaranteed that we'd all end up blacked-out drunk by the end of the night.

Again, living where I live, it's normal to get drunk. It's a hobby for many of the residents of my city. You drink and you watch the corn grow.

You drink and you farm. You drink and you watch football. You drink and you watch NASCAR. You drink and you drink and you drink.

So it's not unusual at all to see, on any given night, a number of people drinking at any one of the fine establishments the town has to offer. It's more expected, even, than it is likely.

It's perfectly okay for people like my parents to go to any bar or restaurant any night of the week and eat and/or drink. They act the same way and possess the same demeanor when entering and exiting the place. They don't fall out of their chairs. They don't throw up. They don't shatter their wine glass. They don't pass out at the table/on the toilet/in the front yard. They don't engage in questionable/risky sexual behavior. They don't do any of that stuff. The thing is, my friends and I would do all of that. It started to become pretty regular. I was becoming a little concerned with my drinking, but I silenced that inner voice that crept into my consciousness. It was convenient to find people who, many times, exhibited behavior like mine. Then I could say I didn't have a problem.

Except, if you're someone feeling this way, before long (unless you die first) you can't ignore that inner voice anymore. I couldn't. That inner voice went from whispering to me, to whispering a little more regularly and urgently, to screaming at me. *Sara, snap the fuck out of it and stop the fucking drinking before you completely fuck up EVERYTHING!*

(My inner voice really likes the f-bomb.)

The point is I was lucky. I consider myself very lucky. I didn't kill myself or anyone else in the process of being drunk, and I easily could have. Like, scary easily. I really consider myself a cautionary tale. I feel guilty when I hear about people who did go through terrible, horrible things that I managed to escape, and I wonder why.

Once again, one thing I'm really starting to believe more than ever is that everything happens for a reason. And even if I don't understand why or how, I do feel that's true. This whole thing has also reinforced my belief in a higher power, even though I don't totally understand that either. I do believe there is something up there, out there, in control of all of this. For me, there's no other explanation at this point.

I had thought the previous summer was the craziest summer of all. I had spent so many nights up drinking until the wee hours of the morning, inviting complete strangers to come hang out at my house, doing all-around irresponsible shit, that I was thinking at that point I might be an alcoholic. I went to an AA meeting with a friend and left thinking I was nothing like those people. The whole meeting itself made me want to go out drinking afterward. I figured I'd just had a bat shit crazy summer, and I was fine.

Boy, was I wrong. Because then came the next summer.

The following summer was the craziest of crazy. Andy had gotten a job offer in Savannah, Georgia, and I was having zero career success here, so I couldn't wait to move off and start anew. I had my hopes up. I was ready. We spent our summer days swimming in our pool, having a few beverages, and then I'd have friends over at night who brought more beverages, and sometimes other items for recreational use.

We usually got wasted and had fun; we didn't care what happened. Some of the time we ended up naked in the pool - one of my friends drove home that way – though she shouldn't have been driving at all. None of us in the group was capable of making any important decisions on any given night. We were all so drunk and/or high that the next morning's realization had me, and I assume everyone else, feeling very fuzzy on the memories.

There were several incidents this summer that kept snowballing, and they all involved me. And alcohol. And men. Not a good combination for me. It's not that I ever intended on doing anything to hurt Andy, ever, but putting myself in those situations, it was bound to happen.

Andy was becoming accustomed to my coming home after a night out drinking and spilling my guts about what I remembered, feeling horribly because I'd blacked out for most of the night and really wasn't sure what had happened. I was always very sorry. I still am. I always will be. I've always turned into a wild party animal when it comes to drinking, I want more and more and more, and I want to have fun and get crazy. It wasn't okay with him. It wasn't okay with me, either, which is why I was always so hard on myself whenever I got myself into situations that hurt my marriage. But it kept happening.

The vodka-soaked straw that broke the camel's back (something like that) happened when I went to our friends' house one night to hang out. As always, we all had plenty of booze. My friend Kevin started passing out some of his prescription pills. I've never met a drink – or a pill – that I didn't like. This was the beginning of the end. Before we knew it we were all laughing, and I was flashing everyone. And this is where it gets blurry for me.

Everybody's rock bottom is different. Some involve DUIs, some involve car crashes, some involve jail time...

Some involve bubble baths.

I have some vague recollections from this night, but I was completely blacked out for almost all of it. I remember flashes of skin. Bubbles. Lots of bubbles. A few friends decided to take a bubble bath together and apparently experimented a little. It happens. Right?

I didn't leave their house until after 6 in the morning. We were still up drinking when Kevin's alarm went off for work. It was Friday. Adele had school. All the kids had slept over at Kevin and Cathy's house, and now I had to drive my kids home. I didn't remember anything. I was still drunk. It hadn't registered, though, that morning meant sobriety and going home. I was still in and out of blacking out, and this is the main reason I will never drink again. Not so much that I don't ever want to hurt my husband again, which is true, but because as I was trying to carry Eleanor to the car, I must've lost my balance and fallen – into rose bushes – it was both of us. I didn't even know it. The next day I was horrified to see red scrapes and scratches up and down her leg and wanted to know where they came from. I noticed I had them, too.

Adele had to inform me, "Remember Mommy, when you were carrying Eleanor to the car, and you fell. Then you got up, and you fell again?"

I did not remember.

I felt like the most useless, worthless, piece of shit parent alive.

I got home and told Andy what I remembered, then I called Dr. M., bawling, telling him, "I think I need to…go somewhere. Like stay somewhere and get help." I didn't know what to do. I wanted help. In between sobs, I told Dr. M. what I remembered from the night before, and he calmed me down a little and told me to let him know how I was feeling a little later, after I'd had an in-depth conversation with Andy.

I think I was hungover for a few days after that bender. Once all of the alcohol had left my system, what I had to do was clear. I couldn't do this anymore. I couldn't keep doing this.

The Light

And the day came when the risk to remain tight in a bud was more painful than the risk it took to blossom. ~ Anais Nin

Today is the day. I want to remember this day forever.

The day I decided to stop drinking.

The sunrise was beautiful this morning. Possibly the best one I've ever seen. Pink and blue hues in the sky sprayed with just the right amount of clouds, the brilliant orange sun barely peeking over the fall trees, as if uncertain of making its appearance.

There are knots in my stomach. I can't breathe (allergies). I am on my period.

I am incredibly exhausted from being awake all night, tossing and turning and trying to banish the unwanted thoughts that kept racing through my head, taking up space where happy memories should be.

I look like absolute shit; my face is broken out, there are heavy purplish bags under my eyes, my hair is frizzy and disheveled. I am wearing an oversized Nike sweatshirt belonging to my husband, stained because of me, a constant reminder (as if I need one) of how I've continually let him down. But not again. Not again.

Not *ever* again.

I am terrified. I have never been in control of my own life, never been in the driver's seat, always a passenger, always letting someone else or something else take the blame. I can't do that anymore. I can't live like this anymore. I can't.

I joke around a lot when talking about drinking; I exaggerate when I've had a bad day and say things like, "I want to drink my body weight in alcohol," and it's funny. I'm being sarcastic and it's funny, and everyone laughs. Except it stopped being funny. I can control myself some of the time, which is why it's been so easy to rationalize why I continue to drink, not to mention that I live in a town where drinking is practically mandatory, and raging alcoholics are accepted with open arms. I blend in here. Alcohol is socially acceptable. It's the times that I don't stay in control that outweigh the times that I do – those are the times that, at this point, have accumulated to an incredible number that I don't even want to think about. It's killing my marriage. If this were reversed, I'd have left Andy by now.

I have used alcohol as a scapegoat, every time. I could do anything with it. I could be invincible whenever I wanted - do, say, or act however I pleased when the numbing liquid flowed through my body. If I offended someone, "I was drunk. That's not the real me. It was alcohol." If I did anything bad, it was the reason. I've relied on it. It has been a friend. A friend who's always been there for me, no matter what. And breaking up is hard to do.

I am absolutely shaking with fear that I won't be able to do this, that I'll fail. I'm ashamed. I'm embarrassed. I'm hurting inside. Badly. I'm so very sorry for the things I have done to people I love, afraid that they won't accept me even if I quit drinking, afraid to become who I really am instead of who I am with alcohol. I don't know the real me anymore.

I have never been so scared in my life.

I'm afraid to face the truth and push denial out of the way, because to do that means I was wrong all these years, wrong for thinking I was okay, and wrong for thinking I could control myself. To admit that I was wrong means all those years, all those incidents shouldn't have happened, and that means I have regrets. And I want no regrets. I feel guilty. I feel like a scumbag. I'm open about *everything* in my life, including my depression (which drinking exacerbates) but this, for some reason, ties my stomach in knots. I'm so afraid of what people will think. Alcoholism, I feel, is looked at by many as a weakness, a sign of making bad choices, not necessarily a disease, even though it's been proven to have genetic predisposition involved, as is the case with me and my family.

Of course, depression runs in my family too, and I have obviously been self-medicating for a long time now. It's the first thing I reach for, my go-to, my trusty friend. With a glass of wine I can feel good again. It's a great feeling. It's the nights that the glass turns into two glasses, then a bottle, then two bottles…the nights I've blacked out, remembering little, if nothing, about a majority of the evening, wondering what I said, what I did…who I did it with…the horrible dread of trying to recall the next day, what took place the night before, the hangovers lasting days – those are the reasons I want to quit drinking. At this point there are no benefits.

But mostly it's my marriage I want to save. I have an incredible man and he does not deserve this. There are a couple of other reasons too, and it's a knife through my heart to hear them ask why Mommy won't get out of bed. No, it's not every day. It's not even too often at all in the minds of many, I'm sure. I know there are so many people who are in much more advanced stages of alcoholism than I am. But this is not their life. This is my life. And I know I have to do this if I want to keep it. I want to be a better wife. I want to be a better mom. I need to be a role model.

I know in my gut, with every fiber of my being and pound on my body, that this is the only solution left. I've tried limiting drinking to weekends, drinking only at home, drinking only a certain kind of alcohol, drinking only for a certain number of hours – I've tried everything. I've taken "breaks" from drinking before when I've been spiraling out of control; I've "slowed it down." But once I started again, I ended up right where I had been. I know I can't just "take a break" this time. I know my addictive, all-or-nothing personality, and telling myself I can stop for a while and then set limits once I start again does not work. I've tried that. It's a slippery slope. I've exhausted the options, made the excuses, and fiercely embraced the denial with a warm, tight hug every single time. This is it. This. Is. It.

I am very scared. What do I do? Can I still have fun? Will I fit in? Will I always feel awkward now? Do I attend AA meetings? I've always thought of alcoholics as people who get up in the morning and have to drink. People on street corners with tattered clothing and bottles hidden in brown paper bags. People who in general seem much more "out of control" than I am. I've never thought of myself as "one of them." As it turns out, there is no exact alcoholic profile. I am one of them.

I'm not sure where to go from here, how to go from here. My path has not been marked out yet. I know that I do need to go from here, though, and take the path I have never taken. In order to save my marriage, my family, *my* life, I can't stay on this path. My therapist said just as much a few weeks ago, when I had, once again, vowed to be better. Yet somehow, some way, no matter what precautions I try to take, no matter how much I worry and think, and *try*, really, *really* try...I somehow always take a detour, and I'm back on the old path again. That path has now been blocked off, eradicated, and filled in with the grasses and weeds of yesterday. I know I have a problem.

So today, I am going down a new path. The path of sobriety. It's surreal. Alcohol has been such a focal point in almost everything I do. It's very hard to imagine my life without it. It might not look like to others that I even have a problem, but I know I do. I'm scared that people won't be supportive, and I'm scared to be this honest and vulnerable. I don't know exactly where I'm going yet, but I know where I've been, and if none of it had happened then I wouldn't be where I am. And that is at a point of great change. Everything in my life has led me to this point. Everything.

My name is Sara, and I'm an alcoholic.

The Sobriety Diaries

One day at a time, sweet Jesus. Whoever wrote that one hadn't a clue. One day is a fuckin' eternity. ~ *Roddy Doyle*

(10/16/11)

It's my ninth day of not drinking and I realize it is hard. I'm very restless. I can't sit still at all; my arms and legs are tingly. I'm too exhausted and achy to really do anything else, though. This is weird. It's better than the first four days; I couldn't sleep at all. I was awake for the most part of four days straight – with whatever this is, along with a sinus infection. My head was pounding and I couldn't breathe at all. My mouth was dry as a desert; I was mildly shaking. It was awful. So now I'm trying to figure out what "this" is and when it goes away. I've been prescribed Campral, which I started taking yesterday. I'm hoping it saves me. I've also really wanted to be "touched" for whatever reason. Like Andy and I have had sex twice and it was amazing. It's like my sense of touch is amplified. I just want to lie around and make out or have sex with him. Sex has never felt better. (Did you know that it's not a requirement to have a glass of wine in order to have sex with your husband? Who knew?) I'm present again. I'm there. Everything is so intense, almost like I just lost my virginity (except it lasts longer than 30 seconds, which is the approximate amount of time it actually took to lose my virginity). This is just one of the amazing side effects of sobriety.

On the "downside"…

We got into a fight last night. We were at a party, which was drinking central, and I was obviously not exactly looking forward to it. I was feeling emotional. Andy was trying really hard to be nice and make me feel comfortable. I wanted to cry. He never knows what to do with me when I'm in that state, and I don't know what to tell him to do.

I'm trying to understand this, understand how I can possibly keep this up forever – *forever* – but it freaks me out when I think of that. Andy says to focus on one day at a time, which is like impossible for me to do. He keeps reminding me he did this for a few months a few years ago, and I keep reminding him that we're different people. That was part of the fight last night. In the end, I came downstairs on the couch until he finally stomped down and said he's sorry if I'm mad at him. Those fights are so stupid, yet they somehow seem necessary.

I can do this, right? People do this all the time. Every day. It's not like I was totally addicted or something, right? Maybe this is mostly mental. Why are my arms and legs so restless, and when does that go away? It's really irritating.

So what do I miss about drinking? Well, it's easier to say what I don't miss. I don't miss being mean to Andy, calling him names and hitting him, things I apparently did sometimes, with no recollection the next day. I don't miss taking a walk the day after a binge, and hearing "Sober" by P!nk on my iPod, and crying behind my sunglasses because it was true; this song was about me, and I wanted to stop. I wanted to stop but I didn't know how.

I'm not sure when I'd say it had gotten completely out of control. I was drinking pretty much daily, starting earlier and earlier, even putting Kahlua in my coffee sometimes. Filling a water bottle with wine to pick up my daughter from kindergarten.

Yeah.

When I wasn't drinking I was on Xanax or Ativan. I constantly needed something to get me through the day, to get me through life. I needed like 27 different pills to sleep at night, and that still wasn't enough. I'd pump my body full of everything and lie there, wide awake, wondering what in the fuck was left to try. Wondering where I go from here.

I hadn't felt anything, really felt anything in God knows how long. I'd been using something, some sort of substance, from morning until night, every single day to make it through. Every. Single. Day. I see that now. I understand now why and how I've been having withdrawal symptoms, even though I'd told myself I wasn't that bad, I wasn't bad enough for withdrawal symptoms, for Christ's sake.

Except I was.

I decided to go cold turkey (where the hell does that expression come from, anyway?) with alcohol, Ativan, Xanax, Ambien, everything. I stopped taking everything. My doctor said it was completely understandable why I was having withdrawal symptoms after being on all of this for so long – longer than I'd realized – and then simply stopping it. At least I did stop this time; instead of convincing myself yet again that the light was yellow while speeding through. I finally acknowledged a red light. I quit everything. And then...

I didn't sleep for four days.

Maybe an hour here or there. But basically, I was awake four days straight. Andy said, "Like a meth-head, you'll eventually crash. You'll have to." Great. So we were comparing me to a meth-head now. Looking in the mirror at myself after not sleeping for four days, though, I have to say...meth-head was probably a compliment.

(10/30/11)

I am super sensitive lately. Andy got a card in the mail from my grandma, who is not doing well, and she forgot to sign it. He said, "Heh. Your grandma forgot to sign my card."

"Heh?" I asked. "That's not funny."

"I wasn't laughing. I never said it was funny."

"You did laugh. If it wasn't funny, then why did you laugh?"

"Sara, stop it; we go through this every time; that's how I talk. I wasn't laughing."

"But you did. So stop it. It's not funny. It's not funny that she's forgetting things. That she's getting worse…that's not funny."

"I wasn't laughing! I wasn't like HAHAHAHAHA!"

"You're a dick."

"Well, Jesus…"

By then the tears had started to fall, hot and wet, trickling like little tributaries around the curves of my nose and down my cheeks. Our kids, who'd both been immersed in coloring at the table, realized something wasn't right.

"Mommy," Eleanor said, "Mommy, there's water coming out of your eyes."

"Yeah, Mommy, what's wrong? There's water coming out of Mommy's eyes, Daddy."

"I know, honey," Andy said, and then turned to me. "Why are you crying?"

I didn't answer, typical me. This was not goddamn rocket science. Maybe because my grandma might be going into a nursing home any day now, maybe because she might die any day now, maybe because what the kids and I had been working on is a care package for my best friend from college, who had recently been diagnosed with all sorts of health problems, including blot clots in her lungs – the thing that had killed my cousin – maybe I was crying about that too, hoping this wasn't my *Beaches* moment.

Or maybe I was having another general emotional meltdown I'm prone to, like the one I had at the church festival a few weeks back, when I walked into the church to use the bathroom. The girls were behaving horribly. Andy was acting cold and distant, a role he was getting rather skilled at playing. The job offer in Savannah, Georgia, had become nothing more than an offer. I had wanted to move. We both had. At the last minute he said we couldn't afford it. I hated my job and was sort of counting on this move as my ticket out of here, away from the shitty job market and all my problems. I was crushed when he announced that we would not be moving. Our house was still for sale though, "in case" he got another job offer, and also, we were poor. Since I'd lost my full-time teaching job over a year ago, ends were barely being met. By like a millimeter. So.

We were at the church festival, actually, because our realtor was showing our house. I was hungover as hell, the kids were grating on my nerves, and Andy wasn't helping. We walked into the church and he took them to the bathroom. I walked the other way, toward the melody I was hearing permeate the entry. I walked into the sanctuary and there was beautiful music playing, candles lit, yet it was completely empty. I sat down on a pew to relish a few seconds of peace before my family would find me. I stared up at the image of Jesus at the front of the sanctuary. I started crying. Tears welling up in my eyes at first, and then really falling hard. Then Andy walked up.

"Are you ready?" he asked. "Why are you crying?"

"I – I don't kn-know," I sort of wailed/whispered.

"Mommy," said Adele, "Mommy's crying maybe because of this sad music. Are you crying because of this sad music?" she asked, wide-eyed, putting her arm around me.

"Um, yeah, maybe," I laughed through my tears, wiping them away. I looked up at Andy. "I just...I wanna go h-home," I choked out, really starting to bawl.

"Okay," he said. "I'll take you home."

I'm not sure what prompted the meltdown. I was exhausted, depressed, hungover, Andy and I were fighting nonstop. I had no direction or knowledge of my future. I wanted to know what was going on. Everything felt hopeless. I wanted answers.

Andy's innocuous comment about my grandma's card kind of sparked the same reaction in me. So overall, I thought I was becoming happier lately, but the "good cries" were becoming more and more frequent. And when I cry, I cry for too many reasons to list. Andy always wants to know, "Why?" He'll ask, "Why are you crying?" Every time. Over and over. And every time I tell him, "I don't know." I do know, but it's like one of those answers that can't be put into words. The impact of everything hits me at once.

I cry because sometimes it's simply hard to be a human being.

(11/1/11)

I haven't been able to sleep the past couple nights. My least favorite time of day is that indiscernible interval between waking and sleeping, when you're forced to face all the thoughts that you could easily dismiss or distract yourself from really focusing on during the day. It's the time of night before I drift off to sleep, when I say my prayers and simultaneously worry that I've been way too fortunate and blessed to deserve this life; I'm afraid something bad has to happen soon. I think about how it's hard for me to really get close to people, to let all my walls crumble down, especially with the people I love the most. I'm just afraid, I'm so afraid something bad will happen. I worry that I haven't been a good enough mom. I reflect not only on the day, but on my entire life, feeling guilty about what I've done wrong throughout the course of the day, throughout the course of every day.

This is why I'm prescribed sleeping pills.

I envy those people like Andy, whose head can hit the pillow and instantly I hear snoring. I think way too much for that to ever happen. Not in this lifetime. I toss and turn, writhe and kick, attempting to drown out the voices in my head that remind me of all the mistakes I've made; I pray that this elusive, invaluable thing we call "sleep" will please grant me with its presence before my morning alarm sounds.

It's weird, really. I mean, I haven't done anything terrible in months, nothing worthy of my lying awake at night ruminating over, punishing myself. I guess once a masochist, always a masochist. I think no matter how "good" I am, ever, I will always feel this sense of guilt and shame that I've done something wrong and don't deserve this amazing life with the fairytale husband and adorable children. I can never shake the feeling.

I'm in a much better mood overall, but I still have lows. I've been in one lately. I'm on my period, so that's half to blame. While I sometimes want to do whatever I can to have the longest, most fulfilling life possible, sometimes I still wonder what the point is. What's the point of spending all this money on potions and creams to look younger, when we'll all eventually get old and die anyway? Why shouldn't I tan excessively like I used to? Why work out? What's the point? Why not smoke?

And the biggest question of all, when I'm feeling really low and discouraged, is what's the point of staying along for this ride if I can't get buzzed once in a while? Is life alone worth it? Is it that great? When I'm in a decent mood, the answer is easy. When I'm depressed, not so much. Everything is nebulous. Nothing is certain, and nothing feels right. I'm confused. I'm irritated. I'm sad. I'm lonely, no matter who's around, and no matter what they're trying to say or do to cheer me up. When I'm low it all seems hopeless and there's no point to anything. There's nothing that can ever pull me out of this, either, not for the 32 years I've been on this planet. It has to run its course.

I don't even try to "cheer myself up" when I'm in a low. I feed it. I watch sad movies, I listen to depressing music. This is how I've learned to embrace it. I don't even want to focus on happy. I can't. It's inaccessible. Doesn't exist in this state. I'm numb, save for the searing pain that courses through my veins and feels like it's practically ripping my heart out as it beats. I hadn't experienced a low like this in a while, so I'm wondering if I should go back on my medication. But then I feel so numb to almost everything all the time, and I don't want that, either. Sometimes this situation in general feels hopeless; I'll never find the right balance that allows me to live.

(11/6/11)

Okay. Nerves. Are. Fucking. Shot. I want to scream at the top of my lungs and throw things and break shit. My children are so goddamn annoying right now. Seriously. Every last nerve has been grated on. And I'm so glad that Andy's not here because we'd only be fighting, because when the kids are horrible, he makes everything worse. I usually want to punch him. Sometimes I do. But only in the arm. You know. Playfully.

Really, though. Whose idea was it to have these kids? I'm kidding. But fuck. Talk about a test of patience. People do survive this, right? People make it past the toddler years? Right now I want to chug a bottle of anything that'll make me want to do nothing but unspeakable, hedonistic acts of craziness so I can forget who I am. I've been doing yoga. And drinking tea. And cleaning a lot. And anything else but drinking alcohol.

God, it's hard. But I can do it. I can do it. I can do this. Even as I type this and am listening to a fucking toy kitten meow incessantly, stuck on the same "Mew" ten thousand times in a row, even as I feel my nerves becoming shot one hundred times past the actual breaking point, even as I hear the squeaking of sneakers on my hardwood floor as the kids run in circles and fight over this goddamn piece-of-shit stuffed animal for an hour, even as I hear, "It's mine!"

"Give it back!"

"I want it!"

"It's mine!"

"Give it back!"

"I had it first!"

"It's mine!"

My Last Rock Bottom

"It'sminegiveitbackIhaditfirstit'smineginveitbackIhaditfirstit'smineginveitbackIhaditfirstit'smineginveitbackIhaditfirstit'smineginveitbackIhaditfirstit'smineginveitbackIhaditfirstIT'SMINEGIVEITBACKIHADITFIRSTIT'SMINEIHADITFIRSTIT'SMINEGIVEITBACKIHDITFIRSTIT'SMINEGIVEITBACKIHADITFIRSTIT'SMINEGIVEITBACKIHADITFIRSTIT'SMINEGIVEITBACKIHADITFIRSTIT'SMINEGIVEITBACK"MUSTDRINKMUSTDRINKMUSTDRINKMUSTDRINKMUSTDRINKMUSTDRINKMUSTDRINKMUSTDRINKMUSTDRINKMUSTDRINKDEARJESUSHOWTHEFUCKDOPEOPLEDOTHIS???

Even as this is going on, right now, I have to calm my shaky hands, somehow stop my skin from crawling – or at least distract myself from it – suppress the urge to strangle my children and the dog, who growls and barks at everything, worsening the already-beyond-manageable level of anxiety, of knots twisting and turning in the pit of my stomach. I have to not kill every living thing in my house, and somehow work with this. I have to figure out a way to cope when yoga won't do, because the state I'm in only makes me want to throw large, heavy objects at the TV set every time the instructor on my DVD orders me into another downward-facing dog.

I need to find a way to cope.

Everyone tells me I'm doing remarkably well and they're very proud of me. That makes me feel really good. But then I wonder if I really am doing remarkably well, considering how I feel inside. Especially on days like today, when it's all I can do not to walk into oncoming traffic as my kids, oblivious, continue to shriek and scream and cry and wail and whine over a two-dollar cat. On days like today, it doesn't matter. Everything will set me off.

The stage has been set for unpredictable, wild emotions, and anything goes. I'd be willing to bet decent money (although don't trust me here; I have no money) that by the end of tonight I'm bawling into the pantry for an hour, like I did already one night this week, while rearranging canned food, because I honestly had no idea what else to do with myself. And the tears wouldn't stop. It was like an automatic drip.

It started because I was upset with Andy, but it was deeper than that. I hurt. It is hard. It's so hard. And even though I know I can do it, not drinking is forcing me to feel everything so much more, to experience every emotion on such a raw level, in such an authentic way. It's like being born. While I don't remember what it's like to be born really, it seems pretty painful. You're so used to being in this nice warm cocoon for so long, so cozy and warm, sheltered by the world, and then, all at once, you're thrust into this blinding light, propelled into such a big, strange place, one that is full of unknowns and scary situations, dark alleys and strangers with candy.

The adjustment period never really wears off. As much as it hurts to be in this new world, though, as painful as it is…I'd never want to return to the womb. But talk about shot nerves. I thought I was having a bad day during the afternoon yesterday. Then night came.

I asked my parents to watch the kids so I could go to an AA meeting, because it became glaringly obvious that if I didn't get out of this house and away from these kids for at least 60 minutes, I would stab something (at this point most likely the dog, and while my husband's been wanting new slippers, I think he'd object when Atticus came up missing, even if Andy would be shuffling around the house in some brand-new Schnauzer Isotoners.)

So yesterday afternoon was trying. And then, it got worse. I started feeling a little nervous about the meeting and told my parents never mind. As soon as I told my parents I didn't need them, I was doubting this, and I got in the shower, started to get ready, called them back, and told them I was still going to the AA meeting.

I've joined an online "AA" of sorts, and it's been great. I can get feedback from the comfort of my bed with a cup of yummy chamomile and vanilla tea, as I lube up with my nighttime lavender lotion.

I was working up the courage to go to another real, live AA meeting.

I turned up some Journey while I showered, an attempt to tune out the kids and relax. I sang my lungs out to "Don't Stop Believin.'

As I got more and more ready, finished blow-drying, began straightening and curling, mentally dressing myself before I actually dressed myself, I started to get more and more nervous. I made some tea. I went outside for a smoke. I took deep breaths. I told myself it would be fine.

And then it happened.

I lost it.

The kids hadn't stopped being whiny, screaming, annoying, needy, tattling, knives-on-my-nerves, waterboarding-my-psyche, testing-me-to-the-complete-maximum-of-human-stress-level-before-anyone-would-snap little beings– even Mother Teresa would have a breaking point, right? I was trying to get ready and look perfect – pick out the perfect outfit somewhere between "I tried," and "I didn't try too hard." In the midst of these crucial calculated clothing decisions, I was expected to dress my children, who loudly and repeatedly fought me – wailing, stomping, crying, every step of the way. Reasoning was no longer with me. Reasoning had left the building a while ago, most likely around the time that Patience, Rationalization, and Stability packed up and got the hell out of dodge.

I resorted to – beyond merely yelling and disciplining. Screaming. So much so that my throat hurt. I roared. I yelled, screamed, cussed, threw things. It wasn't pretty. I'm not proud of it, like many things in my life. Yet, I sigh once again, because, yes it happened, and I have no one else to blame. My already highly fragile nerves were stepped on too much and with too much force during the course of the day, throw in the fact that I'm terrified of walking into this meeting, and then, the kicker.

"Where are my car keys?"

My keys are always in my purse. They weren't. I'd spent all this time getting ready, this painstaking time, to get out of this house, away from these kids for an hour, even if it meant going someplace potentially worse, (it was a sad situation, really) and now I might have gone through it all for nothing? Some may think, 'So what? So she took a shower. Big deal. What a baby. Shut up. There are real problems in the world,' and I see your point there. But emotions are emotions, and emotions are real, and let me lock you up with my children for a day – the way they behaved this day – and then let me see the sunshine, rainbows, and lollipops shoot out of your ass when you're done. But okay. I'm getting off track.

So my keys are nowhere. It's time to go. My kids are still screaming, crying, whining, complaining, wailing. "This shoe hurts!"

"My shoes are too tight!"

"I don't want to wear this!"

"I want to take that toy!"

"Eleanor took my toy!"

"Mommy! Mommy! Mommy!"

"Moooooooommy!"

"Mommy! MOMmy!" MOM!"

I wanted to kill someone. So instead, I screamed at the kids to shut up, yelled at the dog for barking, threw the entire house upside down (that I had just cleaned) looking for those blessed fucking keys. I flew through the cupboards, throwing shit on the floor, sometimes really chucking it across the room in anger. I opened every kitchen drawer, ripping out its contents, throwing and scattering them like who-the-fuck-cares. I became more and more pissed and bitter that I'd be missing this meeting that I had felt ambivalent about anyway, more pissed because I couldn't find the damn keys and I felt helpless, and more bitter because I had spent time to get ready, and I'd been nervous and excited, and now for what? I needed something to happen now. I couldn't have gone through all of that for nothing – to stay home with the kids! Andy would definitely be getting new slippers made out of the dog when he got home.

I called my mom and somberly told her I wouldn't be meeting them at the church after all. "Did you call Andy?" she asked, thinking he might know where my keys were. I had called, and he hadn't known, but knowing him (and I'd suspected as much when I was tearing the shit out of the kitchen) he did know, and just didn't think. So I called again.

He said, "Hello?"

"Where the fuck are my keys?" (I'm a doting wife.)

"I don't know-"

Click. (Again. Doting wife.)

One more time…"Hello?"

"Where are my keys?"

After ten minutes of his guiding me through every pair of Wrangler jeans hanging from the back of every single door in our house, directing me through the front pockets, side pockets, back pockets, pullovers, "What did we do yesterday? What did we do yesterday; what did I wear?" after all of this tortuous shit, I found my motherfucking goddamn keys in his sweatshirt pocket in the dining room closet – a closet we don't hang clothes or coats in. I was livid.

I called my mom, said I was coming, grabbed both screaming kids, threw them in the car, peeled out, blasted The Doors to drown out my children and calm my nerves, and drove well above the speed limit all the way there. Once there and I watched my parents and children pull away, I sucked down a vanilla cigar in between hasty gulps of Earl Grey from my travel mug. The inhale and exhale of smoke, I figured, could end up being the best part of this night and this trip, so I would at least enjoy that. My throat was already sore from yelling. Now it was doubly sore from the intensity of which I inhaled that cigar. I took the long, last drag, sucked it in, held it, slowly exhaled it, put it out, and walked inside to the meeting.

There were three people sitting at a table in the basement of this church when I walked in. Two men and a woman. The one man was older, with whitish hair and a mustache. He reminded me of Wilford Brimley. The woman was a little older than I am; she had dirty blonde hair tied into a Scrunchie, and an Ohio State sweatshirt on. The other guy was also older than I am, a skinny redhead with nice eyes.

They all said hi right away and I sat down, taking slurps of the hot tea I'd brought with me, burning the skin off the roof of my mouth. A couple more people arrived. Besides the guy with the mustache, whose name was Stan, there was the redhead, Joe, and a big and tall guy, Tony, the woman, Melissa, and a Hispanic guy, Carlos.

Joe began by reading a piece of paper about the group, then Carlos read something else about the group's purpose. "I just found out I'm in charge of this meeting a little bit ago," Joe apologized, "so I don't have anything planned. So I figured we'd just keep it open." He turned to me, "We're a pretty laid-back group."

I felt the knots in my stomach begin to unravel. This was feeling like a place I could belong.

Big & Tall passed me some Keebler graham cracker cookies. "They melt in your mouth," he said.

"You talked me into it."

I found out that Big & Tall's actual name was Anthony, and that he lived in the town I grew up in. I said, "I know I'm new at this, I'm new at the lingo, I'm new at the rules…I don't have a home group or a sponsor yet. I stopped drinking October 8…so I'm…new…at this."

It felt good. It felt especially good, when I was done talking, and Stan said, "There are no rules here." Yes. This is what I need. A place to talk and vent and feel loved and not have to walk on eggshells, afraid that I'll mess up the mantra or guidelines. This was the Care Bear hug I'd been looking for.

They gave me a copy of the big AA book. They told me that new members ought to be handled like frightened animals, gently, with care. They told me that I am the most important person in the room. Stan looked right at me and said, "You are the most important person in this room." It was a little overwhelming, but in a good way. It was so touching. I felt that I could open up to these people here and really get a loving, caring sense of them.

Since the meeting was so laid-back, we all shared a little, listened, nodded. They were scrambling to get me books and pamphlets, explaining briefly what to watch out for, not to get discouraged, writing down some of their phone numbers I can call before I take that first drink. This meeting gave me such a good feeling. They took the time to figure me out and they wanted to help; they didn't judge me based on gender, or looks, or style. I can tell they care. And I will go back to that meeting because I want to go back. I felt very comfortable right away.

Here, they told me to forget about the rules. "The only rule we have here is, you have to be a drunk. And you want to stop." I smiled. I could handle that rule.

All in all I loved the meeting. Like I said when I spoke that night, I had been so pissed, so frustrated getting there because of my kids, and everything, I was stressed to the max. Then on the way there I saw the most beautiful sunset. I think God likes to mess with us, to see how much we can handle – test us – to determine who of us is ready to take on more.

The meeting really calmed me down. Everything people read from and everything people said I felt related to me. It was the perfect fit. Now I'm excited to go back. I'm not dreading it with bricks in the pit of my stomach.

The Meeting

Probably some of the best things that have ever happened to you in life, happened because you said yes to something. Otherwise things just sort of stay the same. ~ Danny Wallace

After the last, positive experience I'd had at the AA meeting, one would assume I'd be as excited to go back as I was when I left the prior meeting. As someone who regularly experiences intense bouts of debilitating depression, though, sometimes the depression is stronger than good intentions.

I didn't want to go. I really didn't want to go anywhere, but I also didn't want to go there. I was content with my sweats and unwashed hair, curled up in the chair staring mindlessly at the TV, waiting for something good to happen. I have learned to embrace these bouts of depression with open arms, and the apathy had settled in again like fog hanging over the city, the way it always does.

I told myself I should do something, I should go somewhere before I really go crazy. I didn't want to. The small amount of energy it even takes to get ready, to shower and blow-dry, and all the little steps in between, it all seems overwhelming sometimes. I wanted to sit there and merely exist.

But I made myself get ready. I forced myself to go through the motions of looking presentable. It pained me every step of the way, but I made myself.

On the way there I started to get nervous. I knew at the last meeting they'd mentioned that many regular attendees were missing. I was nervous the members I'd met already wouldn't be there, nervous of not knowing anyone, but more nervous if I actually did.

Maybe I shouldn't go.

Yet, I pulled up and there were three other vehicles already there, waiting patiently for my Alero to glide in beside them in the allotted lines of the parking lot. I somehow exited the car and pulled open the glass door of the building, following the light to the basement.

What I learned at the meeting is that this is the way it can be at every meeting. Once you find a group you like, the stories exchanged, the emotions revealed, the friendships established, those are all genuine and meaningful. I found my home group.

We are all ages, from all different backgrounds, with various amounts of time under our belts. Some of us are married, some of us are divorced, some of us have grandkids. We are all so different, yet so much alike. We tell stories. Stories of heartache and stories of courage. Stories of regret and stories of overcoming. Stories of loss and stories of love.

The sadness in the eyes periodically changes to happiness, eyes crinkling at the corners in the process. We talk. We listen. We nod. We understand. We encourage. We hug. We tell each other it gets easier, and then take that back, and say maybe it doesn't get easier, but you start getting used to it.

Before it's over, I look down, studying my winter boots on the tile floor…I am so glad that I put them on and came.

On the drive home I reflect on everything that was said. I feel that I've made some new friends. I am torn from my reverie when I hear someone singing aloud to the radio. "Bleeding Love" by Leona Lewis is playing. Suddenly I realize that it's me, accompanying her at the top of my lungs. I have been propelled into a great mood without even noticing.

And it's all because of the meeting.

Finding Myself Sober

Be patient toward all that is unsolved in your heart and try to love the questions themselves, like locked rooms and like books that are now written in a very foreign tongue. Do not now seek the answers, which cannot be given you because you would not be able to live them. And the point is, to live everything. Live the questions now. Perhaps you will then gradually, without noticing it, live along some distant day into the answer.
~ Rainer Maria Rilke

I've been invited to a few wine tastings lately. I haven't gone, obviously. What would be the point? As it is, I feel all sorts of emotions when passing through the wine section of the grocery. It's like seeing great friends you've been through everything with, only instead of embracing and planning your next adventure, you briskly walk by, ignoring them, pretending they don't exist. It's strange. There is a sense of loss, and it's hard to explain. I have been through pretty much everything with booze, and to simply cut it out of my life is emotionally draining. Sure, it's for the best, there's no question there. That doesn't mean it's easy, by any means. It's not.

One thing I've discovered since being on the sober side of the fence is that drunks are annoying. I should know. I just kicked five of them out of my house. I don't miss being a falling-down, sobbing drunk.

I had a party tonight, and it was fun, to a point. There was some drunken drama. Drunken drama I would have definitely been a part of a few months ago. We had the completely-out-of-it drunk, the laughing-at-everything-like-it's-hilarious drunk, and, of course, the sloppy-crying-hot-mess drunk. I've been every kind of drunk. All in the same night, sometimes. Those were some fun nights. (Not really.) Looking back, I hate myself. I hate that I was so annoying and obnoxious to be around, I hate that I cried – ever – I hate that I was so out of it that people were concerned. I hate everything about it. I hate that I puked – something else that someone at my party did tonight. Drunk people really are the most obnoxious, revolting people on the planet when you're sober.

Right now I'm annoyed. There's no other way to describe it. I'm annoyed because I drank for so long, and I'm annoyed to see people around me drinking too much and making asses out of themselves. I want to shake them and scream at them until they realize how stupid and destructive they're being. Getting drunk doesn't help, or solve, anything. It only makes everything worse. It's frustrating that not everyone can see that. That it took me so long to see that.

I'm upset because watching them tonight allowed me to see how I was not long ago. I wish I could turn back time and undo some of the completely wasted days due to hangovers. I wish I could salvage friendships that I'm afraid now are irreparable. I wish I could tell the 21-year-old me not to celebrate that birthday, that there's nothing in that rite-of-passage worth celebrating. "It's all downhill from here," I would have told my 21-year-old self.

I recognized every emotion tonight; I know each one so well. I know the drunken tears, I know how much pain there is with each falling drop. I know the giddy laughter of the happy drunk, and I know the fine line between the two. I almost always crossed over from happy drunk to crying drunk, every time I drank. It sucks to hang out with people like that. It's like a ticking time bomb. I have been both girls, way too many times. I wish I knew every single person I've ever offended and could send them an apology letter.

Why is this substance so worshipped? Why are so many events in people's lives planned around it, centered around it, celebrated with it? Why? What's so great about it? What's great is that I'll never have a hangover again, if I do this right. I'll never have a DUI again, if I do this right. I'll never have to hate myself again, not for being drunk, if I do this right.

My Last Rock Bottom

When.

When I do this right.

There cannot be any more "ifs" in this case. "If" does not exist. It has to be "when." There is no alternative to this solution. Whether I really like it or not, my life kind of depends on it. And I'm beginning to be okay with that.

It's strange to be the responsible one. The sober one at the party. It's a role I'm still getting used to playing. I like it so far, though. It's not only nice to wake up without a hangover, but it's also kind of fun somehow to be responsible, accountable. To remember everything that happened in the night. To not be the girl who's the ticking time bomb, who everyone is waiting for - watching and waiting for to screw up somehow. Nervous, because no one knows when it will happen. Or what will set her off. It's nice not to be that girl. I used to be angry. I thought I had to elicit an extreme reaction from everyone around me, whether it be shocked or not. Okay, usually shocked. I did like to shock people. I still do. My life doesn't depend on it anymore. I guess I was so bored with life – my life – that I needed something to happen. I needed reactions.

Now everyone excites me somehow. I can appreciate the differences in people more now that I'm not drinking. There's another whole world out there I wasn't aware of, and it can be a lot of fun. I like tea. Tea is actually exciting to me, picking out new flavors, trying them. It's replaced beer and wine. I do mourn the loss of seasonal beer - that used to excite me beyond measure. Now I'm excited to go tea shopping.

I also like learning the guitar and playing the piano. I'm working out and doing yoga. I'm learning to crochet. I'm writing. I'm actually doing things besides getting drunk and living through the subsequent hangovers. And it really is so much more fun and fulfilling. I can still be sarcastic. I can still unleash 5,000 f-bombs a day if I want. I can still talk about, and have crazy sex. I can still smoke my delicious flavored cigars on the back porch, clutching my oversize cardigan around me as I wave to the neighbor who's raking his leaves. I can still use my wine glasses, filling them up with ice cold sparkling cider as often as I want.

I haven't given up all my vices – and I won't – I've only given up one. But that one has literally changed everything else. I could never picture my life without it. I never tried. It never even crossed my mind. Then one day it hit me. It wasn't even my choice. It was beyond my choice. It was bigger than me. It's like something in the universe saved my life. I believe in God now. I always have believed in a higher power, but I really don't question it now. Will I morph into one of those people who start quoting the Bible? No. But I do think I've had a spiritual awakening. I also believe in karma. I always wondered if that was real, too. I think that it is. I definitely, if nothing else, now more than ever, believe that what you put out into the universe is exactly what you'll get back.

And I want to get amazing things back.

The Diagnosis

At first it's bliss. It's drunken, heady, intoxicating. It swallows the people we were - not particularly wonderful people, but people who did our best, more or less - and spits out the monsters we are becoming.

Our friends despise us. We are an epic. Everything is grand, crashing, brilliant, blinding. It's the Golden Age of Hollywood, and we are a legend in our own minds, and no one outside can fail to see that we are headed for hell, and we won't listen, we say they don't understand, we pour more wine, go to the parties, we sparkle, fly all over the country, we're on an adventure, unstoppable, we've found each other and we race through our days like Mr. Toad in his yellow motorcar, with no idea where the brakes are and to hell with it anyway, we are on fire, drunk with something we call love. ~ Marya Hornbacher

Somewhere in the midst of quitting drinking, I found out I am bipolar. I'd been misdiagnosed once before, or maybe I should say, not adequately diagnosed. I'd gone to a psychiatrist at the time, who didn't let me speak beyond a couple of syllables before scribbling a non-helpful pseudo-diagnosis. This time, however, I'd gone to my counselor who had me complete a lengthy test. It showed that I am bipolar (with borderline traits, as the two overlap in many ways, as far as symptoms.)

It makes so much sense. It explains a lot about me – the bouts of depression, the instances of pure glee for no apparent reason, the want for more, more, more, higher and higher, the pressured speech. The reckless, spontaneous behavior. (Like the time I bought an albino Burmese python on a whim.) I've never been able to do anything in moderation. I know I can't drink. I know I can't shop in moderation – I'm learning. When I'd tan, I'd have to lie out in the sun all day…then go to a tanning bed, twice if

I could…then use self-tanner. Smoke by the carton, or not at all. Be celibate, or…well, like that would ever happen.

I go to extremes. All or nothing. Go big or go home. Super healthy or super self-destructive. No in-between. I'll always be working on it. So being bipolar explains a lot about my behavior, my feelings, my moods. It's a relief, in a weird way, to be diagnosed, because now at least I can do something about it. I'm still working on figuring out the right medicinal cocktail for me. So far it's been rough. I'll be on something for a while and sometimes it's working great, and then it bottoms out and I'm suicidally depressed.

It seems like other people have it so easy, like they don't have to worry about these crazy moods interfering with their daily existence – they're normal. I want that. But then, this is all I know. This is normal for me. Looking back to childhood, even, this all makes sense now.

I wonder what it's like to always want to wake up in the morning, to not look forward to lying in bed and doing nothing else, nothing at all. To cry for no real reason for hours at a time. To lie curled up in the fetal position in your walk-in closet, in the middle of hanging up clothes, because it all suddenly appears to be too much, too overwhelming and too unimportant to be bothered with anymore. To sob as your husband strokes your hair and holds you, and tries to understand even for a millisecond what it's like. To feel as though the razor-sharp pain will never end, even though deep down you know it will; it always does, but to have that suspicion creep in again that this time it really will never end. In a state of depression, there is no hope. There is no future.

The least challenging, most mundane tasks of every day require too much effort to even try to perform, to have every part of your body ache and hurt with every step you take and every breath you breathe. To feel tremendous guilt that you don't want to play with your children; you love them so much, more than anything, yet you simply cannot drag yourself out of bed. To be confronted with the knowledge that you know you're performing subpar as an employee, as a friend, as a mother, as a wife. And yet there's nothing you can do about it. All of this is normal to me. I hate it. I hate that I feel like I've failed most of my life to be the person I should be, to measure up to my potential. I realize most people don't understand, and they never will. I don't blame them. I don't understand it, either. I wish I did. Maybe if I did, then I could change it. I could "snap out of it" like so many people I know think that I can. If only it were that simple.

This, compounded with my sobriety, has proven to be extra challenging. Extra painful. So painful. The drinking took my depression away, even if it were temporary. Now I need to deal with it on my own. And that's hard.

Eyes Wide Open

Facts do not cease to exist because they are ignored. ~ *Aldous Huxley*

I've been up all night with a sick kid and my own scattered, intruding thoughts. It's so strange yet such a relief to know my diagnosis now. I've felt this way my entire life, but I thought I was normal, just a little sensitive. It makes so much sense. I have to say, when I'm on the brink of mania, I look like shit. Or vice versa. No sleep, no makeup, no shower. It always happens when I'm completely sleep deprived. I shoot headfirst into a manic episode and I can't control my thoughts; they're so fast that I can't keep up. I avoid mirrors during this time, and wear my glasses a lot. They mask the under-eye circles. It really is the worst feeling, even though it's exhilarating. It's like driving down the road and knowing that any second you could veer into oncoming traffic. You don't want to, but the knowledge that it's a possibility is frightening, yet exciting at the same time. Like being next to the stove with the burner on high, knowing you could lay your hand there if you want to. Of course, maybe I'm weird and the only person who thinks in these terms. But the ideas – one races into my mind and then is replaced by another one too fast for me to fully comprehend the first one. I write everything down during these times, as if possessed. It's like I have to. I have to or else this all-consuming uneasiness preoccupies me. And once I'm propelled into this state, usually due to lack of sleep, it exacerbates it, and I can't sleep even more. My thoughts are too constant, too vivid to let me rest. I love it and hate it.

It's hard to imagine that not long ago, I didn't want to live. Waking up each day was more than a chore. I hurt all over. The pain of simply existing was too much for me. I loved my family too much to kill myself, but I didn't care if I died. I knew there was a chance, with my reckless behavior and everything I was ingesting that I might not wake up one morning. For me, at that point, it seemed the only feasible answer.

I didn't see how I was benefitting my kids, my husband, my students, my friends. All that would be missing would be me at the dinner table every night, asking the kids, "Isn't Daddy a great cook?" as they enthusiastically nodded. What did I contribute to any relationship I was part of? I was a burden. A "put-up-with" sort of person. Someone you might avoid if you saw her coming. I didn't like me anymore. I had become someone I didn't like – let alone love – someone I'd never be friends with, someone I'd certainly never marry. What was the point of living?

What was the point?

I didn't want to live; I didn't want to face another day. The idea of it was too brutal and made me want to instantly bawl my eyes out – and I did. Repeatedly. When I did finally drag myself out of bed, I watched the clock carefully for a time that I thought acceptable to start drinking. That time got earlier and earlier every day, obviously. I had to catch a buzz. The only thing I looked forward to. I had no will to live. It's very hard to imagine now, almost impossible, but there it was, every day. All day. It had been going on so long that I can't even remember when it started. I was merely existing in this all-around cloud of depression, my body a mere shell designed to encase my vital organs that, to my annoyance, continued to keep me alive day after day.

And then it all came crashing down.

I have been doing yoga for the first time in at least a year, so that's progress. I'm thinking maybe exercise should be my new addiction. God knows I can't afford to do much else. I miss my shopping addiction. Those were the days. I'd wanted no secrets going into our wedding, so I told Andy ahead of time that I had some credit card debt. I didn't even want to say the number out loud, so I told him to guess. I died laughing at the number he hesitantly spit out. I only wished it were that low.

Ah, but gone are the days of manic spending with no regard for the repercussions. I still have it in me, but I no longer have any credit cards, so that, luckily, makes the habit a little more difficult. I'm not sure where my addictive personality comes from. Sure the hell not my parents, and I've been suspecting since about age five that I'm adopted. I'm not, although I'm still skeptical. They're both Republicans with an affinity for Jimmy Buffet. Where did I come from?

"Moderation" isn't in my vocabulary. I'm trying to learn it, though. I always wonder why I can't partake in things like normal people. Instead of buying one thing, I'd spend a thousand dollars. Online. In five minutes.

When I came clean about my drinking, I confessed to my dad that I had taken his Vicodin one time when I'd been at their house. I had no idea why it was prescribed to him, and I'd been carefully eyeing it every time I came over like I would a shiny new bracelet I had to have. I noticed that he wasn't taking it at all. Eventually I swiped the whole thing. (Yeah, so maybe I was worse off than I thought.) When I told him I took it, his response? Wait for it. "What's Vicodin?"

"Ummm…are we related?!" I asked/exclaimed, baffled. Got to love my dad.

But that's my problem. Unlike my parents, I can't "sit on" a bottle of Vicodin without taking the whole thing. I can't have a reasonable amount of alcohol. I want more, more, more. I wonder why. One time I was talking to my mom about this, asking her why I was nothing like her or Dad, and she said, "You're like my dead Aunt Lois. She was a depressed alcoholic. But really funny."

I know that I can't teach right now. For many reasons, it's completely destructive to my entire well-being, at least at the moment. I never really feel confident doing it. I've always tried to fake it, though I'm not sure how successfully. I'm hoping that one day I'll be doing something that I actually am confident in, and I won't have to kill myself pretending. I guess I've always been struggling with trying to get my inside to match my outside. My mom's always said that the state of my bedroom when I lived at home reflected my emotional state. My bedroom was always a complete mess. Disastrous. Kinda like my walk-in closet is now. Even when I clean the house and make it look immaculate, don't you dare open a closet. Shit will fly out and knock you the fuck over. It's like I'm always trying to keep up the appearance that everything's fine, even though below the surface, it's obvious it isn't. It's much easier to shove a bunch of baggage somewhere and slam the door than to actually take the time to sort through it. That's too painful and time-consuming.

Something else I've always had a hard time with is having patience. I used to love (I still do, actually) this song called "Patience," about Herbert the snail, who reminded all the other insects that patience is a virtue. I sing it to myself sometimes when I'm in traffic and feel road rage coming on. But I have huge issues with patience. I want instant gratification. Results. Now. I focus on the destination, and not the journey, and I need to reverse that. It's hard for me. Of course, maybe it's hard for everybody, but other people are better at hiding it.

Things are good, though. It really is how everyone says, one day at a time. When I think of the whole picture and try to plan out the rest of my life, I get freaked out as hell and want to throw in the towel right now. When I focus on the day, my breathing slows down.

I do feel as if now that I've stopped drinking, a cloud has lifted. The last few years have been so foggy much of the time because of all of the times I was drunk. My memories aren't too vivid. I'm excited to make memorable memories again. I'm happier. It's weird; it's still surreal and crazy, and my skin still crawls every day, but not all day. My anxiety is down, and I've stopped the Ativan I was prescribed months ago. Just don't take away my tea, though, or else somebody is getting cut.

I'd still like more answers, like what am I meant to do with my life, but I'm trying not to dwell on it. One day at a time.

Anyway, Andy does like the fact that I'm a "morning person" now, although I think I will never be a morning person, just maybe now someone who happens to wake up before noon. He said, "It's good to see you in the morning. I haven't had that for the last four years." That made me feel good, especially since I feel no one should have to see me before noon, or makeup.

I am glad that I'm getting into a routine, no matter how up-in-the-air everything still is. And, like most other things in life, I didn't try for this to happen. I've simply been waking up early on my own, and the first thing I want to do is write. It's like emptying my brain from the night before. It feels good. It feels as if it's beyond my control, like it's something I have to do. It's involuntary.

I'm really not sure, kind of like the way I felt after having kids, how I lived life before becoming sober. Everything is so much clearer now. I mean, in a way, everything is much less clear, because I think with every ounce of clarity comes more and more questions, like the Don Henley line, "The more I learn, the less I understand." But that's what's great about it. It's so much better to have questions if they're good, important questions, like where is this all going? What does it all mean? What does life mean? Those questions I ask myself sober are much better than the questions I asked when I drank, like, "Did I have sex with anyone last night?"

I'm becoming more and more fascinated by chemical dependency and why certain people are more prone to it. My aunt told me the other day that two more of our relatives were alcoholics. Jesus. God pray for my children. Now that terrifies me. I have a feeling I'm going to want to fast-forward right through the teen years. My mom still reminds me every day of what a bitch I was. It'll be interesting, that's for sure. I can't wait.

There were signs all along. Signs I missed. Signs that got stronger toward the end, so I had to work twice as hard to ignore them. Drinking was such a pivotal component of everything I did, that it did become impossible to imagine having fun without it. The times that I did have fun without it – a lot of fun – I wrote that off as coincidental, one-in-a-million, not-gonna-happen regularly territory.

One time that stands out, that has always stood out since it happened, was the weekend I had to spend at a hotel taking alcohol education classes because of my DUI. I loved it! I seriously had so much fun. And we were learning about alcohol. And no one was drinking. I didn't understand why I was having such a great time considering these conditions. It's like we all bonded, especially my roommate and I. She was there for a DUI, but her boyfriend had driven her daughter drunk and almost killed her. I guess it was a pretty bad accident. That, along with all the dated movies we were shown, the group activities we participated in, and the discussions we had, that's all really impacted me and haunted me since. It was an eye-opening, life-changing weekend for me.

It wasn't enough to get me to completely change my ways. My DUI didn't happen to be my last rock bottom. It was one of them, for sure – it sucked. But it sucked in a different way than several of my other rock bottoms, which didn't necessarily include driving or potentially damaging anyone physically. No, most of my rock bottoms involved – and no big surprise, considering what a "feeling" person I am – emotional pain. I've hurt Andy physically at times when I was drunk, behaving belligerently, hitting. But that's nothing compared to the emotional anguish I caused, though it was unintentional. I honestly never intentionally set out to hurt Andy, or anyone, with anything I did while drinking. That was not my intention. Yet it kept happening, again…again…and again…that's when it was time to take a long look in the mirror.

The second memory that stands out to me, that I think was a sign to stop drinking, happened not long ago at all. My friend Carrie had invited me and a few other girls to her house for a party. I, of course, had planned on drinking, but that was before a little incident happened at an establishment in town, and so Andy and I decided I shouldn't drink anymore without him. The party was going to be all girls, so we tossed around the notion that I could have a little wine, after all, it's all girls! The thing is, though, no one is safe with me. I am a highly sexual person by nature (comes with bipolar territory) and alcohol completely magnifies this trait. I turn into a crazy hedonistic animal. When drunk, if I wasn't throwing myself at men, I was making out with girls. I also happen to be married to one of the two men in existence who does not get turned on at the idea of two women together – he gets jealous. And I didn't want to try and pace myself with the wine, fail miserably, make out with a girl, and let him down again. So I decided not to drink.

I have to admit, it felt very odd at first. I felt uneasy. Normally I'd have been drinking right away, actually, pre-drinking at someone's house before the actual party. Alcohol loosens me up, gives me confidence. I always thought I was funnier when drinking. As I'm starting to realize, people aren't funnier when drinking, they just think they are being funnier. The filter is gone. Mine's already gone, so what the hell?

So this dinner party had given me a little anxiety. First of all, I'd be sober. Second, I hadn't talked to most of these girls since high school and didn't know if we'd have a thing in common or a thing to talk about. Overall I was worried that the whole situation might be uncomfortable.

These girls and I did come from different backgrounds. I've never been in an actual fight, or jail, but they all had. And every story was so hilarious! We spent the whole night laughing our asses off. I hadn't laughed that hard in maybe, ever. My cheeks hurt. I had no idea what to expect going in, but I had a blast – the hands-down best time I'd had in a very long time. And I didn't have a drop to drink. And later, I thought about that. I thought about that, and I was also reminded of how much fun I had at the DUI weekend. I really scratched my head wondering how and why. It never occurred to me to stop the damn wondering and stop the damn drinking! Never crossed my mind. That would've been insane! Now I don't see how I could have missed all these suddenly translucent signs. I couldn't. I couldn't yet. I wasn't ready yet; it wasn't time. I hadn't hit my last rock bottom yet.

This is getting easier, yet more difficult at the same time. I'm really starting to see what a focal point alcohol is around here – everywhere – but here, really, because, well, it's where I am.

I've had to be straightforward with more people lately, when I turn down booze, and they don't get that I really mean it. Instead of, "No, thanks," I've had to say, "No. I don't drink. As in, ever. I go to meetings." Then, finally, they say, "Oh! Really? Wow. Well, good for you!"

I do miss alcohol. I actually miss some specific drinks. People will mention something, and then I realize I'll never have these drinks again. Never. Again.

I miss Guinness. Guinness and I have had some great times together. So many people have always been shocked/disgusted at the idea that I love Guinness because it's so thick and "heavy." And delicious. The foam. Ah, the foam.

I also miss my wine. I love my wine glasses. They're huge. I loved filling them up with plum wine, which tastes like chocolate-covered cherries. Mmmm. Or Spiced Apple from a local winery. It's so amazing. I loved every kind of wine. Sweet, dry. Red, white. It didn't matter.

I also miss seasonal beers. I lived for fall when all the pumpkin ales came out. God, I loved those. And then the winter lagers. Such a great thing to look forward to.

While I was never a huge liquor drinker, I did like tequila. And margaritas on the rocks, with salt. And Long Islands. And Disaronno. That was the only liquor I could drink straight, on the rocks. It was amaretto-y and yummy.

I used to spend the most time in the alcohol section of the store than in any other section - browsing, deciding, choosing, changing my mind. So not drinking anymore does save me time at the store, and through all this, I'm trying to remind myself that the taste of these things that I think I might be missing is only secondary, probably, to the feeling the beverages provided me with. I found a black cherry sparkling water that tastes pretty close to plum wine, maybe even better. So I think I thought I loved the taste of everything more than I really did. I loved how it made me feel.

While I have been kind of mourning the loss of some of these tried and true "friends," I have to remember all the times they weren't my friends, the times they stopped being my friends and betrayed me, again and again - the times they made me feel like shit, again and again. I have to focus on that. So far, the sparkling water hasn't aided me in doing anything stupid or anything I regret. I haven't woken after drinking too much of it, with a pounding head and fuzzy memories. This is good.

It's funny. We watched a movie recently. A comedy in which all the characters get drunk one night and do things audiences laugh about. What I kept noticing, though, were the emotions going through each character's mind the next day. The same shit I used to go through – they kept asking themselves, "How could this happen again?!" That was exactly the way I used to live. Get wasted, do stupid shit, wake up, not remember, ask myself that question, do it again. At one point in the movie, one of the characters is undergoing some real self-loathing (also common for me) when another character convinces him that he, too, is constantly doing crazy shit when drunk that he doesn't remember, and just doesn't worry about it. It's normal. It's cool. Don't beat yourself up. I can't count how many times I'd go sobbing to friends and they'd say the same thing. "Don't beat yourself up. We all do it. You're normal." I realize this is a comedy film I'm talking about here...but it does mirror the way a lot of people live. I'm noticing more and more how the media says it's okay. It's cool. It's funny. It's laughable. When it's your life, though, it's not always so laughable.

It hit me again this morning. I was listening to a song, and the lyrics go into this crazy night involving streaking, shopping sprees, threesomes. Hahaha. It's not a laughing matter – sorry to be a buzzkill – when it really happens. It's fun to sing about…but I've been there. You can describe it in as sing-songy a way that you want. You can dress in 80s wear while you're at it, but in reality, Friday nights like that would, and should, end you up in AA.

I realize not everyone reads into every song or movie that comes across the radar. Every little piece of pop culture doesn't require an in-depth analysis and stern scolding for promoting overdrinking and making light of it, but I am seeing everything in a new light now, almost like it's for the first time. And I do think in many ways, various forms of media make light of addiction. Set it around a fun plot of friends, or to a catchy little beat, and alcoholism is fun! I think in some ways it could be reinforcing a lot of people's negative behavior, making them think they don't have a problem. Maybe I need to lighten up. This is how I'm starting to see some things.

Giving Thanks

I may not be where I want to be but I'm thankful for not being where I used to be. ~ Habeeb Akande

The night before Thanksgiving. Everyone who's anyone is out at the bars right now. It's always been the busiest night of the year, seemingly, for that. College kids are home, everyone's in town. It's time to get out, see people, and get drunk.

I was always one of the many people out on this night, the goal being getting wasted, really trying to forget about how shitty you'll be feeling the next day when all the relatives are mercilessly thrown upon you. Besides, there'll be a shitload of comfort food for the hangover, plus plenty of booze for the hair of the dog. It was perfect. Tradition.

Especially during those post-college Thanksgiving Eve nights out…like any other night out, you don't know at the beginning of the night where you're necessarily going, who you'll be with, where or with whom you'll end up. It was exciting in that respect. Stupid and dangerous, looking back, but exciting. It was so much fun to get all ready in the bathroom, blaring Bruce Springsteen and perfecting a smoky eye while anticipating who I might run into or what might happen that night. The possibilities were endless.

Once we actually got to a bar, it was so packed no one could move. Despite this, everyone somehow made it back and forth to the bar more than enough times to get sufficiently shitfaced. During these times of singledom, I generally "hooked up" with a guy pretty much every time I went out. Not necessarily a different guy every time, and not necessarily sex, but, still…

By the time you'd squeezed your way through the bar and talked to the people you wanted to, most everyone was planning the next stop. Each bar following the initial meeting place always got smaller, darker, and seedier. And closer to someone's house, where whoever was still looking to party could crash and do what – or who- ever he or she pleased.

Ah, yes. The one-night-stand. A staple of my drinking days of yore. So many stories. While I miss the excitement of not knowing who I might be naked with at the end of the night, the excitement ends there. Casual sex was not good for me. It could be fun. But only that night. Not so much the next day.

For many years I thought I was content bar hopping and bed hopping (okay, sometimes couches, sometimes cars) but there is so much more to life than that. At the time, I thought I was having a blast with the one-night-stands. At the end of it, I was all, "Don't give me your number; like we're ever going to talk again." No. No. No, no, no. This never happened.

It was also super fun to get tested for STDs routinely. Those were the days. God, I miss the simpler times. Tests at the free clinic then the bar to drink with my friend and contemplate our results. Good times. And risking my life for what? Some guy – a stranger – who'd provided me with maybe what I'd consider mediocre sex. No. What's the level below "mediocre"? Horrible? That might be it. It was some impressive life I was leading. I'm lucky to be here to tell about it.

So tonight, on Thanksgiving Eve, while crazy kids get drunk at the bars and have sex to regret later, I am home in bed with my tea and my children, texting my husband, who is at work.

And I am so, so thankful.

Black Friday . . . Indeed

There were days when she was unhappy, she did not know why - when it did not seem worthwhile to be glad or sorry, to be alive or dead; while life appeared to her like a grotesque pandemonium and humanity like worms struggling blindly toward inevitable annihilation. ~ Kate Chopin

Today I am unmotivated. Empty. Lazy. Kind of sad. I'm not sure why. Nothing bad has happened. I even did some online shopping today. No way in hell was I going in public with those batshit crazy Black Friday shoppers. Still, I feel hollow. I've been feeling pretty good – really good – most days. Maybe I'm feeling emotional. Yesterday was Thanksgiving, and I was around a lot of family who were drinking. I made it through, but I still can't say it was easy.

It hasn't been easy. I sort of feel like I might be on the verge of another good cry. As well as it's going and as good as I feel, there's still a lot of pain underneath. And I've been trying to make up for lost time with the girls by playing more, but I still have tremendous guilt for the time lost being drunk or hungover all those times. Every time. I know it does no good to dwell on it, and I try not to, but sometimes it happens. I want to be a good mom.

I think days like today are necessary, though, as much as they can suck. Complete happiness can't exist all the time, or how would we even measure happiness? I'd been so used to not experiencing this feeling of loneliness and emptiness lately that maybe a small part of me wanted to believe that was gone for good. I know I am still human, though, and that I'll always have days like this.

From quitting drinking, if it's been an indication, these days will be fewer and further between, which is good. I haven't had the feeling of wanting to die since I quit. I think that's a good sign. I think I've been feeling so high-as-a-kite happy that today is unfamiliar territory now, instead of the norm, like it used to be. And that's great. I need some coping mechanisms so I don't lose hope. People do always say the best way to cheer yourself up is to cheer someone else up, and I've coincidentally been dealing with quite a few drunk, sobbing, depressed friends lately. It's so ironic to be the one on the other side. I know now that days like this won't last forever, and I've been through much, much worse. I can do this. Even if days like today feel as if there's a slight gaping wound in my heart that can't be filled, there isn't an amount of money in the world you could pay me to cross back over to the other side where I came from.

Sometimes, like today, merely existing is painful. I find myself pacing around the house, not sure what to do with myself, feeling so restless and ambivalent at the same time. I have zero motivation to shower, change clothes, try to look presentable in any way…no impetus to really do much of anything. Only I have to do something. Even though I haven't felt this exact way in a while, the second I feel an ounce of the familiar sadness seeping back in, it's like being in labor. You forget how painful it is to give birth after the first kid, until you feel that first contraction with the second baby. Then it's like, holy fuck, now I remember how much I hated this. Like being strapped into a rollercoaster seat, you're already click-clicking your way up the first big drop and it's way too late to jump off now. That's how I feel about life sometimes. As much as I've maybe thought about ending it on more than one occasion, I'd rather ride it out. Like roller coasters, so far it's been worth it to get past the first uphill panic attack.

The thing I know that's been helping me virtually every day is writing. Writing for me has been more therapeutic than sex, than exercise, than talking to friends. It's the thing that really makes me feel better. I feel super anxious and crazy until I get onto the page what's been bottled up inside me, and as soon as I let it out, it's such a rush. I've read that people with bulimia feel anxious and on edge until they purge, and then everything's right in the world again. That might be kind of a dark and disturbing analogy, but from the descriptions I've read, that's how I feel about writing. So basically I just compared my writing to vomit.

I won't lie. Winter is going to be rough. I can already feel it. I'm pretty sure I have Seasonal Affective Disorder as it is, and to me, especially, it's always been "winter equals wine." It goes hand-in-hand to sit by the window and watch the snow fall with a glass (okay, bottle) of wine. And now I'm feeling the shorter days and fewer hours of sunshine (as unsunshiney as I might be) having an effect and I need to find something to do with myself. In the summer, at least, there are more ways to be distracted – taking walks, sitting on the porch swing, sitting out by a fire…in the winter, you sit inside. With your children. What the hell am I going to do?

I can tell that alcohol withdrawal is making me cranky. I hung out with a friend recently, and she was like, "Okay, so I'm dying to know how it's going! How are you doing this? Don't you crave it?"

"Fuck yes I crave it!" was my logical response. "It's hard as hell."

I'm not sure what answer she was expecting, like I decided to quit drinking and some magical switch was flipped so I don't want to drink anymore. I want to drink all the time. I want to drink right now, so badly that I can't believe it. Some days are better than others. Today's been hard. Sometimes I really wonder if I'll be able to do this. I can type away all night, sipping my sparkling cider, but there'll always be that something missing. That void that only alcohol can fill. Sweet, amazing, pain-numbing wine.

I miss it. I miss the end of the day when I could lose myself in a giant glass of Riesling, feeling the nice, relaxing buzz within minutes. Everything became easier; nothing was forced. Everything became languid. I naturally wanted to talk about whatever came to mind; there were no sober, awkward silences. Now, instead, I have a sharp, stabbing pain in my chest where the buzz used to be, a symptom of the anxiety that comes and goes as a result of taking away this addiction.

What I have to remember is that what's the alternative? There is no going back. We've established that I'm not someone who can drink a little. To try that would mean going back to getting wasted, fucking things up with my marriage, living through the Hell-on-Earth hangovers and suicidal depressions that accompany those, and I can't do that. I won't do that. It's not even an option. So when I'm feeling sorry for myself or in so much pain that I think I could die because I need the taste of alcohol, I remember how much worse I felt when I drank. And then I shut the fuck up and try to focus on the next distraction to keep me sober.

While I know I have friends and there are days my phone is ringing off the hook, days like today mean I'm scrolling through my contacts list, calling anyone and everyone, in desperate need for someone to pick up and prove I'm not alone. But even then, it's not enough. No one who isn't going through this understands what I'm feeling. Andy tries, but he'll never get it. I don't blame him for that; it's the way it is. Sometimes it's a matter of doing whatever possible to get through the day and get ready to face the next one, hoping it's better and easier. Honestly…

I WANT TO DRINK SO FUCKING BADLY RIGHT NOW I COULD SCREAM.

I'm hoping by tomorrow morning that sentiment can at least be expressed with a little less urgency. These are the little goals I shoot for. They're what keep me going. One day, one goal at a time.

The After Party

Bad times have a scientific value. These are occasions a good learner would not miss. ~ Ralph Waldo Emerson

I got a job at a gym. I know, I've expressed my thoughts about gyms. But I'm desperate. I need money. Plus, maybe I could develop an exercise addiction and feel better about myself.

So right when I started, they had a Christmas party. It wasn't so great. I don't know these people very well, and being the only non-drinker (and the drinkers were real drinkers) I did feel a little uncomfortable. I was feeling vulnerable and introverted. I've noticed that I'm much more introverted since I stopped drinking. I hear, "You're quiet" a lot now, and I never used to. I heard it tonight. I was offered drinks only about ten times, which I politely declined, but it got old. Andy, who is always "on," was definitely "on" tonight. He's loud and likes to be the life of the party. Everyone thinks he's hilarious and I'm often not in the mood. I live with him. All of his jokes are new material for everyone else, but I hear them all 30 times a day. I was annoyed. I was more and more annoyed the drunker he got. Especially when he promised me this would be his "last one" and then we'd leave, until, of course, until someone else handed him a beer and he promptly cracked it open. Then everyone looked at me like the party pooper and disapproving wife. "Trust me!" I want to scream, "I was the life of the party. I'm not a buzzkill; I just don't drink now, and it's not so fun watching everyone around me get wasted and obnoxious!" Andy's sense of humor involves lots of sexual innuendo, as does mine, but I guess I wasn't in that mood tonight. Especially when he talked about "sticking it in my ass."

My boss was at this party.

I felt so disconnected from him, so completely annoyed by him, like we're not on the same team. I hate that. I want to be around him and want us to be on the same page, and when we're not, and he's forcing me to roll my eyes out of annoyance or embarrassment, I don't want to be there.

Then, on the way home, he was drunk and told me to turn the wrong way, then got us completely lost and was blaming the GPS, which we hadn't even been using. He yells all the time when he's pissed (which seems to be often lately) and yells at me, though he says he doesn't try to. "Well, I tell him. Then don't. Don't 'not try to; just don't do it." But he still does. I don't even feel like talking to him now.

Okay. What happened after the drive home Sunday night was horrific (at least emotionally). Andy went completely nuts. He wouldn't shut up. I was ready to divorce him on the spot. He'd seemed sober when we finally found our way home, so he drove to his dad's to get Eleanor. Well, he must not have been sober, even though he promised me twenty times he was okay to drive. God, I'm really starting to fucking hate alcohol. He came home and was completely pissed off because he'd been like two hours late to get Eleanor and that was met with a little pissed-offness of its own. (I knew it would be which is why I'd been trying to get his drunken ass out the door at the party for half an hour). So when he got home he was yelling, screaming, pacing around, repeating himself because he'd gotten chewed out. This, of course, prompted him to crack open another beer, which he definitely didn't need. His eyes were all crazy and I was starting to get a little bit afraid of him. I hadn't seen him this way in a long time. I told him beyond ten times to seriously shut up. I wanted to leave.

Finally, as I had been lying in bed using the laptop while he sat next to me screaming, I'd had enough, so I threw the damn computer off of me and stomped out of the room, slamming the door behind me (the doors really slam no matter what; it's an 110-year-old house and everything's wood). I practically ran to the couch where I curled up in blankets and tried to will myself to pass out so I wouldn't hear him anymore. What I did hear was his clambering down the stairs toward me. He ripped the blankets off of me and shrieked at me for throwing the laptop at him. Of everything he said, the thing that sticks out is, "Even when you were lying on the ground in town with your legs spread, I didn't throw anything at you!"

Wow.

So that was referring to one of my drunken mistakes, a night I barely remember, a night I certainly had never described to him in that way, as I had tried to piece it together after the fact. Well, he must have put it together that way on his own, and when he said that, that hurt. That really hurt.

He finally trudged back up the stairs and passed out, I assume. I don't know. I cried myself to sleep.

The next morning he came downstairs before taking Adele to school and kissed me on the forehead. I pretended to be asleep. The second he left, I got up and got ready to go to twelve hours of training for my job. When he got back from her school, I left right away, ignoring him when he said goodbye.

We text messaged back and forth all day while I was at training. My stomach was in knots the whole time. I knew he was really sorry, and he didn't mean any of what happened the night before. I believed him. We basically "made up" via text, which is strangely the method we usually use for making up. It doesn't allow either of us to keep going on and on and drag everything out longer than it needs to be. I mean, I wasn't done talking about it, but we covered a lot.

He does better in messages than he does in speaking, I think. He has a tendency to verbally fuck up a lot. When he writes, everything seems so eloquent and sounds the way I wish he always sounded when talking. It's weird.

So anyway, we got over that. I mean, I wouldn't say I was "over it" completely. It was pretty bad, and I don't understand what the hell got into him. I'm willing to bet it was the large quantities of liquor he was dumping down his throat, though. And it's not like I can't forgive him, after everything I've done. This really puts it in perspective, in another way. It sucks. It really sucks to be shit on by the person you love. It shakes you to the core and threatens your whole security system and makes you at least temporarily question everything. It's not fun.

He promised to not drink liquor anymore. I also said he could stand to slow down on the beer, that he doesn't really need eight Yuenglings on a week night when we're home with the kids. Everything has put booze in a whole new light for me since I've stopped drinking.

I kind of think of it as poison now.

Breaking Up Is Hard to Do

The feeling is less like an ending than just another starting point. ~ *Chuck Palahnuik*

The thing that I'm learning more and more about alcohol, the further I separate myself from it, is that it is not a friend of mine. Sure, I've thought of it as a friend many times, and I suppose it has been. But overall it hasn't been. And that's what I have to focus on. I was talking to a friend's husband yesterday, and he's been sober eight years. He says it gets easier with time, but that it also can be really hard from time to time. He compared it to the death of a loved one. At first it's excruciating, but then it gets easier, and then it's almost an afterthought, until you have those really bad days when it feels as if the loss just happened again. Of course, with the death of a loved one, depending upon who it is, I'm not insinuating that it's ever just an afterthought. Maybe just that it's not the focal point of your everyday living anymore. It starts to not consume every single thought throughout the day.

Being sober allows me to see everything clearly. I notice everything more. Everything having to do with drinking, especially, I'm hypersensitive to. I notice how many people actually do it, how much they drink, how hungover they get, how they keep on doing it anyway, again, and again, like I did.

My senses are all so heightened since I've become a spectator, and not a participant in the sport of drinking. I used to only be absorbed in myself, and losing myself in my own drinking. Now I can seemingly hear the *Tsss!* Sounds of beer cans opening from miles away. The *Pop!* of wine being uncorked rivals the deafening roar of a cannon being shot off.

And the smells - the smells cause me to instantly salivate and nervously bite my lip, chew on my fingernails, twirl my hair, and wonder if everyone else, preoccupied with their scotch, gin, or pinot grigio, can sense my panic.

Whenever I've been in social situations like this, where I've been so used to drinking in the past, I take deep breaths and remind myself that I can do this. This is nothing. I can do this; I can survive this. I focus, again, on the crippling, debilitating hangovers. I remind myself how productive I've been since I quit drinking. I tell myself I know everyone is so proud of me. To let myself down would be letting all of them, down, too. I think of my kids, of their sad, tiny, disappointed faces that used to stare up at me when I couldn't get out of bed and come play with them after a night of drinking.

I imagine myself getting divorced.

All of this mental imagery allows me to breathe a little easier. There's no doubt I'm doing the right thing. I know the ethereal "high" alcohol can provide is also ephemeral. Like mind-blowing sex with a partner who you know otherwise is no good for you, it can be so, so good, yet how long do orgasms really last? Is it worth it? No.

I now notice how much time and energy is put into alcohol. How people plan events, their weekends, their nights around it. I know I used to. I look around, the morning after, and feel sorry for all those people who feel like shit. It seems so silly to keep engaging in a behavior that only makes you feel terrible shortly after. So silly. Yet I completely get it. It's about that time in between, the time of imbibing, and the feeling that you're on top of the world and untouchable. It's protection. It's a force field. When I was drunk, I was prettier. I was smarter. I was deeper. I was funnier. I was sexier. I was better in bed. I was a better dancer.

Except, I wasn't.

I wasn't any of those things. Drinking doesn't improve anything. It relaxes your mind enough and takes away those pesky inhibitions so that one thinks she is better in every area. Alcohol drowns the self-doubt.

There's a reason it's referred to as "liquid courage." It really works. Sobriety is scary because it forces us to face the truth. The unaltered, unclouded, unimpaired truth about ourselves. How scary is that? I was shaking, I was initially so afraid of what I'd discover. Of course, now I know that might have had something to do with some of the physical withdrawal symptoms.

I have been feeling really restless lately. As Dr. M. mentioned a while back, the "sobriety honeymoon" will eventually wear off. I think that might be where I'm headed. I'd been so "up" on making the change, as scary as it is, but I've been keeping myself really busy to not focus on that. Now, it's getting to the point that I can't simply pick up a nice new hobby every day. The fanfare is wearing off and life is stepping in. I need to get into a groove, into a routine now. Talking about making the change is therapeutic, but now I need to really make the change. Make bigger changes that can take the place of alcohol. A guitar won't do it. Crocheting won't do it. Even sparkling cider in a wine glass won't do it.

I need more of a mental, spiritual change, not a string of physical alterations. I need something deeper to fill the hole. I've been throwing insignificant handfuls of junk into a landfill, and now I need one huge, all-encompassing pile to really fill the thing up. So the question is, how do I do that?

To ease some of my restlessness (and perhaps increase it later) I have applied for a credit card. I don't want a huge limit, and I don't want to get back into crazy debt, but I am tired of being poor. I don't even know how I could get Christmas presents otherwise. I feel confident that I can do this without fucking it up. I hope. I'm going crazy here; I need a release. No drinking *or* shopping?

The tea I drink every second isn't exactly fulfilling my every longing. I need a break. So I'm granting myself that. I know that with credit cards, like everything else, that I have a habit of completely spiraling out of control in an impressively short amount of time. I'm trying to keep a grip on it this time. I can't live anymore with no breathing room. I'm really going insane.

Aside from having no money and really feeling the urge to buy something, I think overall I'm feeling okay. I'm settling into this new role of non-drinker. I like it. It's going to be a lifelong adjustment, I think, but so far the challenging aspects have definitely outweighed the way I used to feel before I quit drinking.

I really don't want to mess up again – with alcohol, or credit cards, or anything - so getting a new card does make me nervous. I think I could go even crazier in the long run if I don't. I can't take depriving myself of everything all the time. I'm feeling like I can't breathe. And Andy doesn't get it. He doesn't get *me*. He can try all he wants, and I can explain it to him with as many analogies and metaphors as possible, but he can only understand to a certain extent. He doesn't, and never will, really understand what I'm feeling or going through with any of this. With having addictions, with having bipolar disorder, with being me. Not that we as human beings ever really know what it's like to be anyone else, but at least other people with mental illness can relate to me; other people with alcoholism can understand. That's what I need.

It's also become glaringly obvious lately that there are two types of people in this world: those who understand addiction, usually because they have one, and those who don't. It's generally something people can't understand unless they have the addictive gene. They don't know why I can't have one glass of wine and stop.   Simple, right? "Just have one glass."

"Oh, okay! That's easy! Why didn't I think of that?!" I want to scream in their faces. It's like the people who don't understand depression, and when I'm feeling suicidal, they say things like, "Count your blessings!"

I know they mean well, but after a while, it becomes infuriating. "Really?" I want to say. "How the fuck do you not have your own mental

My Last Rock Bottom

health practice?" At least, this is how I respond in my head. In reality, I'm much nicer to these people, really.

But the thing is, people don't get it. They don't get it, and then they spout off with this ignorant bullshit, leaving no shadow of a doubt of how really uninformed and uneducated they are. I know they're trying to help. That doesn't mean it isn't excruciatingly painful to a clinically depressed person who's been trying for days to feel better, to emerge from this coma of pain, to hear some sing-songy Bible-thumper quote a verse. I've had to refrain from choking someone a time or two. I take deep breaths and remind myself that I don't know what it's like to be them, and they don't know what it's like to be me. And that's okay. It helps to explain to them in very detailed, descriptive terms that what they're saying has absolutely no effect on me or my mood, nor will it ever, and then the explanation of chemical imbalance comes into play. By then they've usually gotten bored and tuned out, after, of course, they've informed me that fresh air always lifts their spirits. Lovely.

I've really noticed the divide more clearly now that I've stopped drinking – there are those of us who spend our lives looking for ways to numb the pain, and those of us who seem to experience minimal pain at all. Those of us who think too much, and those of us who can enjoy a vacation from start to finish, without that miserable tendency to focus on the fact that it will inevitably end, and therefore never be able to truly let go and have fun. I envy those people. The ones who can live in the moment and appreciate it for what it is. It takes work for me to do that. I really have to tell myself not to worry about the future or dwell on the past, because it does no good. My natural inclination is to worry.

It's amazing how changing something that predominantly took place at night can affect my entire day, every day. Because I was becoming crazier and crazier every time I drank, I had to start morphing into that person when I was sober, to prove I didn't a problem. To show that I behaved the same way when I was sober and drunk. Alcohol affected my everything. I think because I used to look forward to the moment I could drink every night that it altered everything I did throughout the day. Now I have to stay busy every second to preoccupy myself and keep myself from even thinking about alcohol. It's not easy. Some days I have no problem finding projects to keep busy. Other days it feels like work and seems to drag on into nothingness. It's a series of dreadful sippy cup filling and potty training disasters, minute by minute, hour by hour, until finally it's an acceptable time to lie down and end what feels like the never ending waking hours.

Sometimes I wonder if I'll go completely crazy before this is all said and done. I wonder how many people have gone crazy from abstaining from something. Is this documented somewhere? Which takes me back to the beginning, and that's "why." Why I quit drinking. "Why'd you quit drinking?" someone will ask me. While obviously I know the answer, it's not a simple answer to give to people, not the sort of neat and tidy answer people are looking for that can be easily repeated and transferred from source to source. "Oh, Sara Berelsman quit drinking. Yeah, it's because she hates the color blue." It's not like there's one reason. Kinda like there was never one reason when people would ask why I was a vegetarian. I eventually started giving a different answer, depending on my mood. I think my favorite was, "I don't eat anything that ever took a shit." (I eat meat now, by the way, in case you were wondering. Why? I got hungry.)

So now, with becoming a non-drinker, I'm sort of adopting the same style and providing a different answer to different people if the topic comes up. Sometimes it's, "I turn into a stripper when I drink (which I do) and that wasn't so good for my marriage," and other times it's, "I black out when I drink (which I do) and that wasn't so good for my marriage." Regardless, the theme is generally that it wasn't so good for my marriage. There is a slew of reasons why I quit, but that's the big one, the headliner.

I've realized that giving up alcohol is a lot like going through a break-up of a relationship with someone. That's why it's hard to pass through the alcohol section at the store. We tend to romanticize everything and focus on the good times and tell ourselves it wasn't all that bad, but.

We have to remind ourselves of all the bad times, of the reason for the break-up.

Day by Day

God grant me the serenity to accept the things I cannot change; courage to change the things I can; and wisdom to know the difference. ~ *Reinhold Niebuhr*

Something I've been thinking about is that my friend is having a party this weekend, and I've been saying I'm going, but the closer it gets, the more I don't know if I want to. I've been feeling so down and emotional lately, especially in social situations. I don't want to go to the party and feel like shit, wishing I hadn't gone. But if I stay home, it means Andy and I might fight, and I'll feel bad anyway. Why is this so hard? Sometimes I wish there were a place I could go to when I want to be alone, to escape, run away, from everyone. Get away. But I don't know what that place would be.

I know that I don't feel overall nearly as depressed as I did when I was drinking, but I have been down lately. I stopped taking my medication for depression, because I felt like it wasn't doing anything, but I'm wondering if I do need it after all. I wanted to check, I guess. I also guess I kind of don't want to think I need it for some reason. I hadn't wanted to listen to any of those depressing songs I go to when I feel like this, not for a long time, but lately, I want them. I need them. I hadn't felt alone and sad like this in a while…but I do now. And I almost feel more alone lately than I ever have. I think because of this decision I've made, to stop drinking, I feel like a freak in some ways. I feel as if so few people really understand. It's like I'm in some little group of weirdoes, of people who don't belong with the mainstream. I don't fit in with people who can handle their alcohol. I'm different. I can't relate to them, and they can't relate to me. It's strange.

I think I'm in desperate need of therapy right now. I was doing fine for a while; it seems that I've hit a wall or something, and now I feel sad and contemplative. Maybe I wanted to think my depression was gone for good. I wanted it to be. Now I know it's not; I was on a long high.

It doesn't necessarily bother me to have to take medicine. I want to know for sure that I need it, that the pros outweigh the cons. I know I can't deal with this down feeling for much longer. It had been gone for so long; it really sucks for it to be back again. I feel like crying. Nothing seems worthwhile right now. Everything hurts my feelings – although I know it's not my imagination that a lot of people in my life have been hurtful lately. Maybe this is some sort of test. Of what? My sobriety? My sanity? I want the sadness to go away.

I have learned more about myself lately, though. Like, I do get embarrassed. For example, that whole incident at my work party, when Andy was talking about anal sex. Someone said, "You're embarrassing her!" Andy said, "She never gets embarrassed!" Well, I actually do.

I'm also an introvert. I sort of adopted this extroverted persona because I did bold, crazy things when drunk, and I think I started to become and define myself the way that others said I was, or said I should be. I'm not all that bold and crazy and talkative. I'm talkative, but not extroverted. I'm a different person now, but I'm more "me" than I've ever been, I think. It's like I'm coming out from behind this curtain I've been behind for years, reappearing for the first time as the person who originally went behind it. It's crazy.

Someone else at the work party said I didn't smile the whole time, and remarked how quiet I am. I told her that I was the loudest person in the room – when I was drinking. I'm not now.

Now, when other people are loud and obnoxious and full of sexual innuendos, I sort of shut down. It's like too much for me. I want some meaningful, one-on-one conversation. With one person. I don't want a crowded bar. I don't want loud drunks. I don't want stupid jokes. I want quality conversation with clear-headed people. Am I boring? Am I not fun? I don't know. But at least I don't regret anything in the mornings anymore.

Some days are better than others.

I don't feel as if I want to jump out of my skin every single day anymore, but some days I do. I still try to occupy myself at all times so I don't think about it. I've rediscovered bubble baths. I've learned to appreciate playing with my kids since it happened.

I am accountable now. I used to be able to justify every one of my actions; I could always blame the alcohol for my behavior. Things used to "happen" to me, as in, "I don't know what happened last night; I was drunk, and {fill in the blank} happened. As if I had no part in any of it. Now I know, I was putting myself in those precarious situations.

I feel alive now. I used to wake up, counting down the hours until I could start drinking. I dreaded the monotonous routine of every single day, going through the mundane motions of living, waiting for the moment to forget about my troubles with the help of some chardonnay or merlot. Or Miller Lite or Guinness. It really didn't matter to me. It all got me to the same place.

I envy people who can drink responsibly and in moderation. I tried. And tried. And tried some more. No matter what I did, however, I always, always wound up in the same spot. I couldn't do it. It took me a long time and staggering piles of denial to figure that out. I must've hit rock bottom at least ten – or thirty - times before I came to the conclusion that in order for me to stay married, keep my friends, keep a job, and stay alive, I had to quit drinking. I never thought I was one of "those" people.

An alcoholic.

That wasn't me. I happened to have a lot of nights with blackouts. That didn't mean anything. Lots of people get DUIs; that didn't make me into someone who needed AA. This is what I thought before I hit my last rock bottom.

I'm understanding more and more every day how wrong I was to deny the problem. It's not normal to have sex with someone else's boyfriend. Or to have sex on the side of the road, against the car, with a guy I just met. To have sex with three guys in one week. To have sex with two guys on the same day. (The overlap between Josh and Alan. It's not like I planned it. And Alan knew I had had sex with Josh earlier that day. Awesome. I might also have a sex addiction.) To end up in the bathroom of a restaurant with a much older, married man. I don't think we had sex, but I was blacked out. I could go on and on...

What?

Did I really do all those things? Yes. It was me. And I didn't want to be that girl anymore. How could I have been so stupid? So careless? So fatalistic? Because I didn't care about myself. It was all porn sex. Meaningless. Completely different from love sex. But I focus on the fact that I do admit it now, and that's what matters. It could've been worse. I have faced my demons. I'd like to think that I can now help others face their own personal demons. I've decided to turn my "problem" into an opportunity.

So now it's about making it through each day, hour by hour, minute by minute, second by second. It's about being able to go to the grocery store and suppress my desire as I bypass the alcohol section. It's about noticing all the things I took for granted when all I cared about was getting a buzz.

It's about rebuilding my life.

I know people say it gets easier with time, and that keeps me going. That and I try to focus on the positives, like the reality that I'll never have a hangover again, or not remember an entire conversation from the night before, or embarrass the hell out of myself in front of anyone. I won't hurt my husband because I was drunk anymore. I'll be in the shape I should be in if there's an emergency with one of my children. I'll be there for my children.

Yes, it's difficult. It is. When I think of the bigger picture, like the idea that I won't be toasting with champagne on New Year's Eve or at weddings, I won't be drinking on my anniversary which is on St. Patrick's Day, I won't be drinking again ever, all of that overwhelms me to the point that I want to give up. Which is why I go back to thinking about it second by second, minute by minute, hour by hour. Every second I don't drink is a success. At the end of the day, I feel good about myself that I made it, and I thank God.

And I pray to God for the strength to make it tomorrow.

A Magical Year

Magic is believing in yourself, if you can do that, you can make anything happen. ~ *Johann Wolfgang von Goethe*

I keep thinking about what this guy said at the last AA meeting I went to. I discovered he'd stopped drinking at age 32, the age I am. "Thirty-two is a magical year," he'd said, shrugging and smiling. I mouthed it quietly, repeating him, "Thirty-two is a magical year." I liked the sound of that. At the time, I was still feeling more positive than I am now. I hadn't hit this wall of darkness yet, this seemingly impenetrable block of doom that's keeping me from feeling any sort of hope out of this despair. I've been trying to repeat this to myself, like it's my mantra, whenever I've been feeling down or discouraged lately.

Thirty-two is a magical year.

I think I thought as soon as I stopped drinking, I'd miraculously be happy. How naïve. Now I'm wondering if I'll ever be happy. I'm losing patience and hope. I'm running out of ideas and distractions and excuses about why I don't feel the way I think I should or the way I think everyone else expects. I am exhausted. Defeated. Overwhelmed in some areas. Underwhelmed in other areas. I feel confused about what I'm supposed to do next and how I should be feeling, and how I should be striving to feel. I don't know this. I don't know any of this life. I need someone to navigate, and I want someone to tell me it'll all be okay, and I want it to be someone I trust, and I want to believe. Is that too much to ask? I want security.

I'm tired of feeling anxious and panicky and like I can't relax in my own skin. Isn't life too short for that? That's not how life should be. I don't want to waste another second worrying about mean girls at work who talk behind my back, or trying to please impossible bosses. This is my life. Shouldn't it be fun? And full of passion? Where is that? How do I change it so I have that? I don't want to live like this anymore. I changed the drinking. Now I need to change more. I'm not happy yet. And maybe the clarity from not drinking is making that more evident.

It is impossible for me to make small talk right now. I can't do it. I can barely talk. I simply don't give a shit. I don't care how your holidays were, and I don't care how your kids are doing in sports. I'm sorry. I don't fucking care right now. It's not you, it's me. I'm sure it'll pass, and I'll (half-ass) care again, but lately, conversation pains me. It literally is painful for me. I can't do it.

Sometimes I look around the gym and wonder why. Why are we all there, like on hamster wheels, sweating our asses off? For what? I don't think this every day, but I've been thinking it lately.

This. Is. Hard. I want wine so badly right now. A glass. A giant one. I want a buzz. I know it'd only make me feel worse, though, and I'm wondering if I'm developing dependencies on Ambien or Ativan, which I'm back on. Sometimes I so badly want to feel good that I know I've abused them a time or two. I don't think I'm addicted, but I miss getting a buzz. It's hard. It's super hard. It's painful.

I need to get back to a happy place. I've been down so long lately, in this funk. I need to get out. I need something to work toward and look forward to, but what, is the question.

There used to be so much more to look forward to when we were younger. Birthday parties, skating parties, slumber parties. Now even going out and seeing anyone is few and far between. I don't feel the need to try to even look pretty almost any day of the week.

That's depressing. I don't see the point. And I haven't come to terms with working out yet and making this big body transformation. I don't really care, to be honest. I'm kind of feeling like resigning myself to the fact that this is my body. I don't love it. I don't even like it, but what the hell. This is it.

Where did all the positivity go I had a couple months back?

My "honeymoon with sobriety" has ended, and now what? Well, this is the "now what." This is the hard part everyone at AA refers to when they say the first year is the hardest. It'll be three months tomorrow. That's huge to me, and at the same time, that's nothing. Three months?! I'm only thirty-two. Can I do this forever?

I won't lie. The suicidal thoughts have been stronger lately. Just thoughts. I'd never have the guts to do it, and I wouldn't want to do that to my family. But I've gotten back to that dark place lately, the place that makes me think it might all be easier on everyone if I weren't here. And, for my sake. I feel empty again lately, and if this is as good as it gets, what is the point?

I thought maybe with the newfound sobriety, I'd have a new outlook on life and be this suddenly positive, changed person. I am changed. But I'm not the effervescent ray of sunshine I thought might eclipse the darkness of my normal persona. And I'm okay with that, I guess.

Thirty-two, I need more of your magic to appear.

Reality Check

Our deepest fear is not that we are inadequate. Our deepest fear is that we are powerful beyond measure. ~ Marianne Williamson

It's the same every time. I start out having a little. A glass of white zinfandel, nothing more; that's all I have. Then I have a little more. Maybe half a glass more. Then a full glass more, until I've downed the bottle, and another. I'm at first giggly and mesmerizing, speaking with ease about poetry, politics, whatever – I am brilliant and eloquent, captivating and mysterious.

Soon the talking turns to touching, and it's innocent, I tell myself. Friends can touch. That's all this is. Nothing more.

Then I'm blacked out drunk, doing whatever it is that my body wants to do, going where it wants to go, following only hedonistic instincts, not in my right mind whatsoever. Of course, I'm unaware of any of this at the time. I'm somewhat filled in by others, clues provided by time and place, snippets of fuzzy memory sometimes racing back in and out of my brain.

Things I don't want to remember.

And then I wake up, startled, dripping with sweat. It takes a moment to register. What's horrifying about these nightmares I've been having is that I awake the same way I did when I would come to my senses after one of those real nights of drinking and not remembering. It would all hit me slowly, one brick at a time, until the whole, heavy pile fell on my chest and I was suffocating; I couldn't breathe at the unthinkable realization of what I'd done, or might have done.

What did I do?

Now these dreams haunt me at night, disrupting my usual enjoyable vivid nocturnal films with the replaying of events in my life, events I regret.

Every time I wake up I am upset, ashamed, that I fell off the wagon. I drank, and I got drunk. How did I let myself do that? And then I realize it really didn't happen.

Why am I having these dreams? Am I just that afraid of failing? Am I thinking a lot about the things I've done that I regret?

Maybe both.

Coming Out of the Darkness

It is better to light a candle than curse the darkness. ~ *Eleanor Roosevelt*

Today I am ten months sober.

I never thought I'd make it this far. As I've repeated over and over and over, it has not been easy. I know how repetitive I sound, but it's true. That should be emphasized.

My job at the gym is no longer. This is a good thing, as it was not a good fit for me. I enjoyed the free spin and yoga classes, but working there, I was miserable. No one ever gave me anything to do, and I need to be mentally challenged. I bawled the day the girl from work sat me down and basically evaluated me to my face, more or less telling me I suck at life. I'd been in a very deep depression, crying every day, really thinking about suicide a lot. I found out a few days later when I got in to see my doctor that it was the medication I'd been taking. I'm still trying to figure out what works for me.

I don't want to have any regrets. I've made bad decisions, many times, but I've also made a good decision – a great decision – a wonderful decision - by deciding to stop.

It's hard. It always will be. But I know I can do it. I'm ready to move toward the future and see what it has in store for me. I'm tired of feeling guilty about the things I've done and the friends who don't want to seem to talk to me ever again. I'm learning that I can't control everything, only myself.

And I'm starting to really like myself.

Instead of feeling indignant or upset about who doesn't like me and why, I feel sorry that they don't have the human capacity to forgive. I'm still learning to forgive myself, and I hope anyone I've harmed will be able to forgive me. If not, I have a great group of people in my life who know everything and who are still there. At this point in my life, the friends who have been with me and stayed with me at the lowest point are the ones I want. This has taught me what unconditional love means.

I write for a couple of newspapers. I also blog for various outlets. I've written about my alcoholism. I have this urge to open up, to let people know who I really am, even if I'm a messed-up, mentally ill person who really does not have her shit together. I'm tired of pretending. It's exhausting. I want to be real. By being real and becoming who I really am, I've discovered that other people respond to that, and they become real, too. It's like my favorite part in The Velveteen Rabbit, the book that brought Andy and me back together. I don't want to be anything but real from now on, even though it hurts sometimes. I've already made some great new friends because I've opened up about being bipolar, and about being an alcoholic. Slowly but surely, the shame, the stigma associated with these things are being lifted. Lifted up and away from me, higher and higher.

Wishing on Dandelions

Believe there is a great power silently working all things for good, behave yourself and never mind the rest. ~ *Beatrix Potter*

I am almost 18 months sober. I thought I was doing great for a while, and now I'm struggling. It's hard to not want to drink when Andy still drinks around me. He's limited it to weekends, but it's still hard. I've been crying a lot lately. We're still figuring out my medication.

My moods have been fluctuating quite a bit lately, and the urge to drink has been quite strong. I'm going to start attending more AA meetings. I want a sponsor. I want a safe haven, a place to go where there are others who understand me. I'm willing to keep trying, maybe get a sponsor, maybe even work the steps. I hear it works for a lot of people, and I'm in a pretty dark place again right now.

But I've faced all my demons. I think we all have them. I've released the skeletons in my closet, and they're probably off somewhere, engaging in questionable behavior. Still. we all have them. Why not share, and help each other? Otherwise, why are we here?

I've still been trying to forgive myself for the things I've done in the past. The people I've hurt. The reckless behavior I've exhibited. I know now that the bad things I've done don't define who I am. They're things I've done. And I'm sorry. I did these things. I wasn't in my right mind and it's not who I am. But I did them.

I've started a depression/bipolar disorder support group. It's been therapeutic for me and it's actually been great. I've had some people in the group say things to me like, "You've changed my life…in a week!" I feel that I'm finally figuring out what my purpose in life is. And I think it's to open up about my "problems" in order to help others. It ends up helping me in the process.

I'll still be taking it day by day, hour my hour, minute by minute. That's all I can do. It's difficult. My kids still remember that night, the night of the rose bush scratches. My last rock bottom. Kids have great memories. But it is another reminder that I am doing the right thing, and how many people I am doing it for.

Maybe the majority of those I drank with were just sad, broken people, and we found each other at the right or wrong time, depending upon how you look at it. I'm still figuring it all out.   Figuring myself out.   Figuring life out.

I want to be someone people can look up to. I don't want my parents to feel like failures, because they're not. They did an amazing job. I'm the one who made the decisions I made. And I think they should be proud of me now. I have a wonderful, supportive husband, and while it's been rocky at times, and we've gone to therapy for that, we are still together. And always will be. Because I don't give up. I won't. I have two beautiful children who I love more than I thought I could love anything ever – *ever* - and I feel really blessed.

I've always believed in honesty. While it's scary, the thought of being judged, it's been so liberating since I've opened up about my struggles. Sometimes it takes a while to get on the right path. It's okay to reach out to other people. It's okay to admit you were wrong. It's okay to be human.

It's also okay to appreciate the little things in life - and looking back, those little things could be big things. I've always loved dandelions. Whenever we take walks, Eleanor picks at least one for me and tells me to make a wish. Whenever this happens, and this might sound weird, it's like a spiritual experience.

I think of dandelions as the "underdog." People call them weeds, but I don't. I got a tattoo to commemorate my year anniversary of sobriety, a

My Last Rock Bottom

tattoo of a puffy dandelion with the word "Faith." I have faith that all my wishes will come true.

In the end, I am grateful to have finally made it here, to have hit my last rock bottom. People always think of rock bottom as being bad, the lowest point possible. While that might be true, there is another aspect of rock bottom that people don't think about. I think of rock bottom now as a good thing, not a bad thing. Had I not ended up there, I wouldn't be where I am now.

If you look closely, you'll see beauty in those rocks at the bottom. Sparkling beauty. And maybe a fluffy dandelion poking through a crack, stretching out, looking upward as the sun's rays shine down, illuminating every tuft. Until someone blows the tufts away and they soak into the ground, growing brand-new dandelions, full of potential. They are beautiful. Even if they are growing at rock bottom. Because they can now start making their way back to the top. And there is light above.

So much beautiful light.

****

"Here, Mommy!" Eleanor said happily, her little outstretched arm tightly gripping a puffy white dandelion. "Now make a wish!" I took the dandelion from her, closed my eyes, and wished with all my might.

THE END

About the Author

Sara Berelsman has a BA in English from Eastern Michigan University, and an MA in literature from there as well. She has taught college level courses in the humanities at several schools over the years.

Her lifelong love of writing led her back to that, as she now writes regular columns for a couple of newspapers in her area. In addition to writing for the papers, Sara also writes the blog and newsletter for a mental health organization.

Her short story, "Answers in an Ice Storm," has been featured in a book which was released in June 2012, *Spectral Hauntings: Anthology of the Supernatural*. A few of her other short stories have won or placed in various writing contests.

Besides writing, Sara enjoys playing with her two young daughters and two rescue dogs, and spending time with her husband. She also enjoys hula hooping, bike riding, listening to P!nk, watching thunderstorms, and being sarcastic. In her free time, Sara has been tossing around the idea of going back to school to be a counselor.

If you liked *My Last Rock Bottom*, please leave feedback.

If you liked *My Last Rock Bottom*, we suggest these Word Branch Publishing books:

When Angels Call: Coping with Grief and Loss by Dr. Maurice Turmel: https://www.wordbranch.com/coping-with-grief.html

Wilding Days by jerjonji: https://www.wordbranch.com/the-wilding-days.html

Real Men Don't Wax by Stacy Bender: https://www.wordbranch.com/real-men-dont-wax.html

For a limited time, get a 10% discount off your entire book purchase from the Word Branch Publishing Virtual Book Shop. Enter the code CD10 at checkout. See more of Word Branch Publishing's books at http://wordbranch.com/book-shop.html.

My Last Rock Bottom is published by Word Branch Publishing, an independent publisher located in Marble, North Carolina. If you have a finished, or near-finished, book, we would like to hear about it. Word Branch Publishing believes that everyone has something important to say. http://wordbranch.com

CPSIA information can be obtained at www.ICGtesting.com
Printed in the USA
BVOW06s1812220915

419155BV00011B/146/P